THE WORLD OF
★ PRO ★
FOOTBALL

Author's Dedication
To Bree, Mona, Sandy and Lewis,
All-Pros in any league.

Photographer's Dedication
For Gin, my second right han

THE WORLD OF PRO FOOTBALL

Photographed by
Manny Rubio
Text by
Paul Fichtenbaum

Designed by Philip Clucas   Produced by Ted Smart and David Gibbon

CRESCENT BOOKS
NEW YORK

CONTENTS

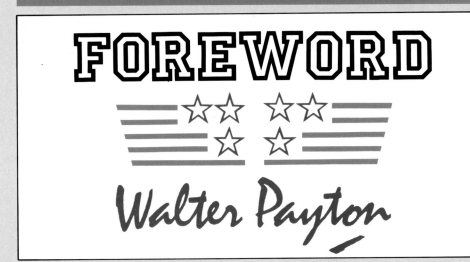

FOREWORD

Walter Payton

If I was asked to sum up what football is all about, I would say "Contact" – either you like it or don't like it.

Contact has to be fun to all participating – the players who are participating in the athletic contest, and the spectators who are viewing it.

We all start competing with each other at an early age. The child on the school ground on a Saturday afternoon playing sand lot football after choosing sides is playing because he wants to be there. The professionals who show up on Sunday afternoon for the Super Bowl all want to be there. There is no substitute. You either want to be there, or you won't be there. Money cannot buy the desire to be there.

I find no difference today in my feelings for football than what I did in high school. If the day comes when I don't get goose pimples before a kick off, then I will be ready to sit down.

So much for the personal aspects of the game. Football is truly a team sport. If the receiver can't catch the ball, the quarterback looks bad; if the line doesn't block, the runners look bad; if the quarterback hands off poorly, the runner fumbles; or if the defensive back doesn't cover the receiver well, the defensive line looks bad.

To play the game, one must enjoy it first; then have the discipline to help a team play as a unit. The blocking, faking and receiving have got to be just as important to the running back as the running itself.

While I never refer to football as work, only as fun, the statement is true.

The famous doctor, lawyer, writer, etc. are all hard working perfectionists. This is true in all aspects of life. Also this is true in football. You work out twelve months a year. When you report to camp, you should be ready to play in the Super Bowl.

It is an honor just to play on the same field that the "Great Ones" played on and coached (Knute Rockne, Red Grange, George Halas, Sammy Baugh, Vince Lombardi, etc.) Their leadership paved the way for fortunate people like me.

Columbia High School, Jackson State, and Chicago Bear fans are the greatest. I could not have done it without their help. The media has also been very supportive, for which I will always be grateful.

Football has given me a life better than I deserve. I have a wonderful wife, two perfect children, financial security and wonderful friends. All of this, for just having fun.

To steal the words from the late and great Lou Gehrig, I must say that "Today I am the luckiest man in the world."

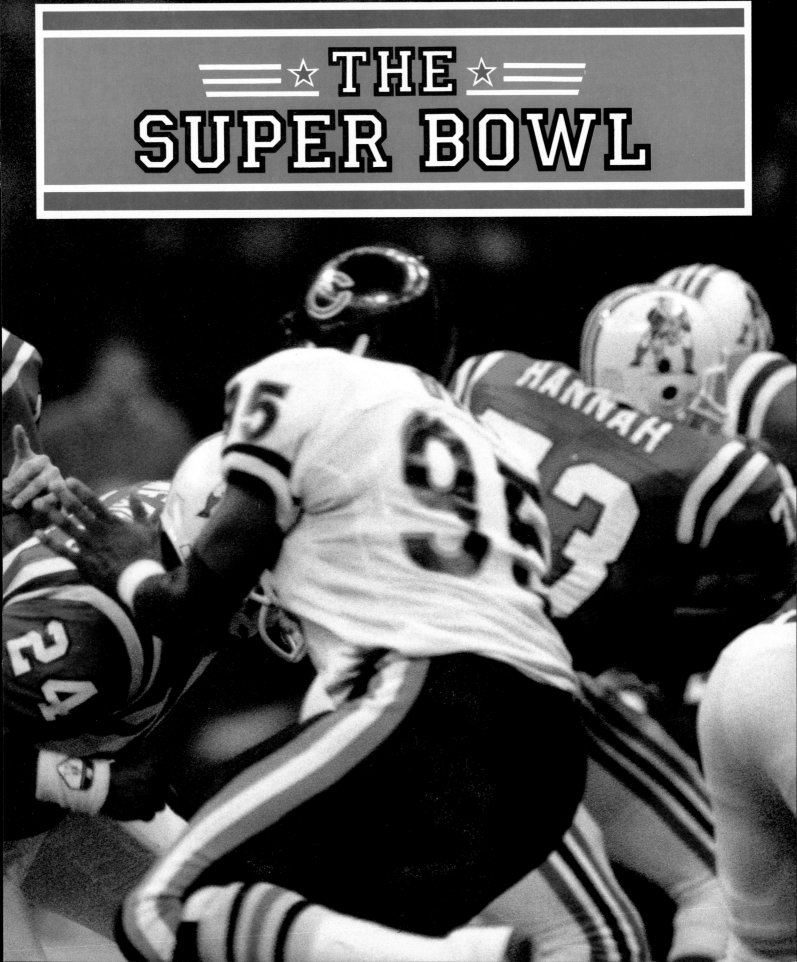

THE
SUPER BOWL

Heading into Super Bowl XX, the Chicago Bears and New England Patriots had taken distinctly different paths to the top.

The Bears, the rough and tumble characters of the Midwest, had partied long and hard, swaggering their way to a 17-1 regular season record. Opponents were not only crushed by the Bears' impenetrable, suffocating defense and underrated, opportunistic offense, but by a volley of barbs not seen in the National Football League since Joe Namath brought his underdog New York Jets into Super Bowl III against the powerhouse Baltimore Colts.

The Bears were bold and brazen, a team of confident, talented players who talked tough, yet backed it up on the field. The week after Chicago's only loss of the season, a 38-24 pasting by Miami on a Monday night, the Bears recorded their "Super Bowl Shuffle" video. And a week before the biggest game of their lives, the Bears gave the Patriots something to hang on their bulletin board, something to rally around. "We want a goose egg," proclaimed Chicago linebacker Otis Wilson. "We want to be the first team in Super Bowl history to register a shut out."

The New Englanders were the antithesis of the Bears. A conservative team held together by a conservative leader in head coach Raymond Berry, the Pats surprised all the experts by grinding out victory after victory in the playoffs to reach the top. First they upset the Jets, then they thrashed the American Football Conference's best team, the Los Angeles Raiders. To complete the trifecta, the Pats bounced the Dolphins out of the Orange Bowl, putting them one victory from an astonishing achievement.

"This makes Alice in Wonderland seem like a true story in comparison," said New England owner Billy Sullivan after the victory over Miami, propelling his Patriots into the Super Bowl.

Maybe he had a point. After all, the only other "wild card" team to reach the Super Bowl was the Raiders, and even the Raiders enjoyed one home game during their run.

Perhaps the Patriots should have considered themselves Cinderella

Previous pages: Jim McMahon (top left) and Kevin Butler (bottom) have the winning look while Steve Grogan (main picture) faces the fury of the Bears' rush. Chicago cheerleaders (facing page top) and Dan Hampton (above) celebrate the victory. The Patriot defense (facing page bottom) take out their frustrations.

instead of Alice. And perhaps they should have gone home before the Big Ball because on Super Sunday, the day of the Biggest Ball of all, the Patriots' glass slippers were chewed, digested and spat out again by the Big, Bad Bears. The final score read 46-10, Chicago, but that is not a true barometer of the beating the Patriots took. Not only will they have to live with the memories of that slaughter in their minds, but on paper, where numerous records of futility were set.

To give a true idea of the utter dominance by the Bears, consider these Super Bowl records: most points by one team (46), largest margin of victory (36 points), most points for a team in the second half (23), fewest first downs rushing (one), fewest yards rushing (7), and lowest rushing average (0.6 per carry). Now consider that New England was the sixth best rushing team in the league, a club that averaged 279 yards on the ground in the playoffs.

"We're the greatest defense ever to play," proclaimed Bears star defensive tackle Steve McMichael. "We just don't think any team can beat us, that's all."

"I know that some of the Patriots took offense at what we were saying," said All Pro safety Gary Fencik. "They thought we felt superior to them. I guess now they know we had reason to believe that."

And how. This was especially true as the game itself unfolded. The normally staid, conservative Patriots opened up their offense with the passing game instead of sticking with the reliable rushing offense. Maybe the Bears defense, which allowed 118 yards rushing in its two previous playoff games, helped dictate what New England would do.

"I wanted to come out throwing. I wanted to get their attention," said Patriots' coach Raymond Berry after the shellacking.

"I was surprised that we didn't run more," admitted New England back Tony Collins. "Our offensive line felt it could run, but it never got a chance to prove it."

The Patriots' first five plays from scrimmage were incomplete passes. The sixth play was the Bears' first of seven sacks on Patriot quarterbacks. "I'm not saying it's right or wrong," said Bears middle linebacker Mike Singletary, "but they went away from what got them here and that is difficult to do this late in the game."

"They tried to lull us to sleep by saying they were going to run, run, run," McMichael said. "Then they come out throwing."

Things looked anything but bleak for the Patriots early, as big-game jitters put a crimp in Chicago's game. On the second play from scrimmage, Chicago's veteran running back Walter Payton fumbled, the Patriots recovered and it looked like New England's luck with turnovers would last one more game. After all, this was a Patriot team that forced a plethora of turnovers in its three playoff games, with two of the contests (Miami and New York) against teams known for their mistake-free offense.

New England, however, could not cash in as quarterback Tony Eason threw three straight incomplete passes. Tony Franklin then came on

and kicked a 36-yard field goal to give the underdogs a 3-0 advantage with only 1:19 gone in the contest. It was the earliest score in Super Bowl history.

"I looked up at the message board and it said that 15 of the 19 teams that scored first won the game," remembers Singletary. "I thought, yeah, but none of those 15 had ever played the Bears."

While nobody could ever accuse the Bears defense of lacking confidence, the offense, though not nearly as dominant as the "D", was equally confident. And not even the

A rusty Grogan (above) took over for an overmatched Tony Eason. Facing page: Kevin Butler (top left) kicks a field goal while Willie Gault (top right) shows off his world-class speed. Quarterback Jim McMahon (facing page bottom) hands off to the reliable Walter Payton.

Bears defense could boast a character in the mold of Jim McMahon, the quarterback with the rifle arm and bazooka mouth.

For two weeks prior to the Super Bowl, McMahon kept his tongue

wagging by commenting about everything from commissioner Pete Rozelle to the Patriots to his wounded rear end, which he insisted needed his acupuncturist Hiroshi Shiriashi.

"I really enjoyed myself this week," said McMahon of his New Orleans McMayhem. "This is a great city. All that crap earlier in the week? Ah, that's life. You just have to put it out of your mind and concentrate on football.

"We wanted to prove that we were the most dominant team in football and we proved it."

Nobody proved it more than McMahon, who coolly brought the Bears back after the Patriots struck first.

On the next series, McMahon orchestrated a 59-yard drive (including a 43-yard bomb to Willie Gault) which finally stalled on the Patriot 10-yard line. Kevin Butler kicked a 28-yard field goal, pulling Chicago even at 3-3. Then the fun started for the Bears defense.

Two incomplete passes by Eason gave the Pats third-and-10. A perfect situation for the Bears to swamp the quarterback. Even before Eason could say ouch, both Richard Dent, the game's Most Valuable Player, and Wilber Marshall used the scrambling signalcaller as a blocking sled, sacking him for a 10-yard loss. According to Chicago, this series of downs was the beginning of the end for New England.

"You could see it in his eyes," Singletary said of Eason, "it was that look that said, 'Oh my, here we go again.'"

It's no wonder Eason may have had a look of disbelief in his eyes. In the first six offensive plays, the Bears vaunted "46" defense showed six different looks. Each time they were effective in shutting down Eason's receivers. When they weren't all over the receivers, they were all over Eason.

"They've proven that they are the best defense I've ever coached," said former Bears defensive coordinator Buddy Ryan, who accepted the Eagles head coaching job after the Super Bowl. "They were mediocre at the beginning of the year, but they clawed and scratched their way to the top."

After the teams traded punts, New England took possession and finally shunned the pass for their specialty, the rush. Craig James, who

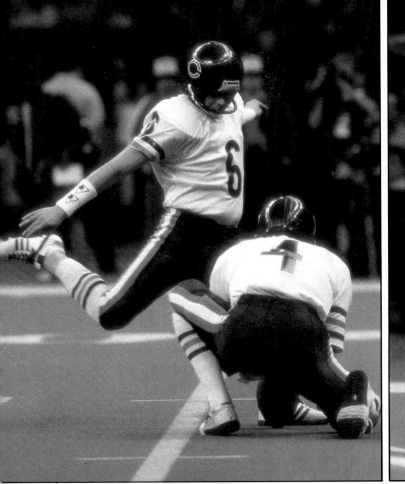

13

gained over a 1,000 yards in the regular season, was stuffed for no gain. Back to the pass for Eason and Back to the Future for Chicago. Dent and McMichael burst through the middle of the line and popped Eason, causing the ball to come loose. Dan Hampton recovered on the Patriot 13 to set up another Butler field goal and a 6-3 advantage.

On the next possession James tried to sweep left, but Dent stripped him of the ball and Singletary pounced on it at the New England 13. This time McMahon's offense punched it in with Matt Suhey scoring the touchdown with an 11-yard run. The score was 13-3, but in reality the game was just about over.

"The pressure (of the defense) just got to us," said New England's right guard Ron Wooten. "If I could do one thing differently, I'd like to go out and challenge the Bears with what got us there, running the ball, but we didn't. Probably we should have. The Bears are just better than we are right now. I'm not embarrassed, I'm humiliated.

"When we couldn't move the ball on our first run I thought, 'Where do we go from here? We can't pass, we can't run.' It was like trying to beat back the tide with a broom."

The only broom that could be found was the one that was sweeping the Patriots back to New England red faced with embarrassment. For the Bears were just getting started.

Before the half would end, McMahon drove Chicago 59 yards in 10 plays, including a 24-yard completion to Suhey. Then just before the half, the Bears QB hit a 29-yarder to Ken Margerum to set up a 24-yard field goal by Butler as time ran out. The half time score: 23-3, Chicago. But it was worse than that.

After several futile attempts to get the offense in gear, Berry benched young quarterback Eason in favor of veteran Steve Grogan. Grogan, who had gone down in Week 12 with knee ligament damage and a broken tibia, orchestrated the offense the rest of the way, but he also fell victim to the ferocious Bears defense.

"I will admit that their defensive schemes are the toughest to attack and deal with," said a despondent Tony Eason after the game. "The Bears are the most aggressive team that I've

Stephen Starring (above) tried to get the offense in gear against Chicago. For most of the one-sided contest, Mike Singletary (facing page) and the Bears looked like Supermen to the outclassed Patriots.

seen this year or any year.

"Our problem was getting manhandled, outplayed. I tried to scramble, but there was no place to go. They played an almost perfect game."

That perfection continued in the second half as Chicago scored 23 more points, 21 in the third quarter, to bring about the most lopsided Super Bowl ever.

"It's hard to describe what this means to the guys who have been here the longest," sait Gary Fencik, a Bears veteran for 11 years. "We've worked so long towards a goal and to have it come true really is emotional. No one can say it is a fluke."

Least of all the Patriots.

15

THE CONFERENCE CHAMPIONSHIPS

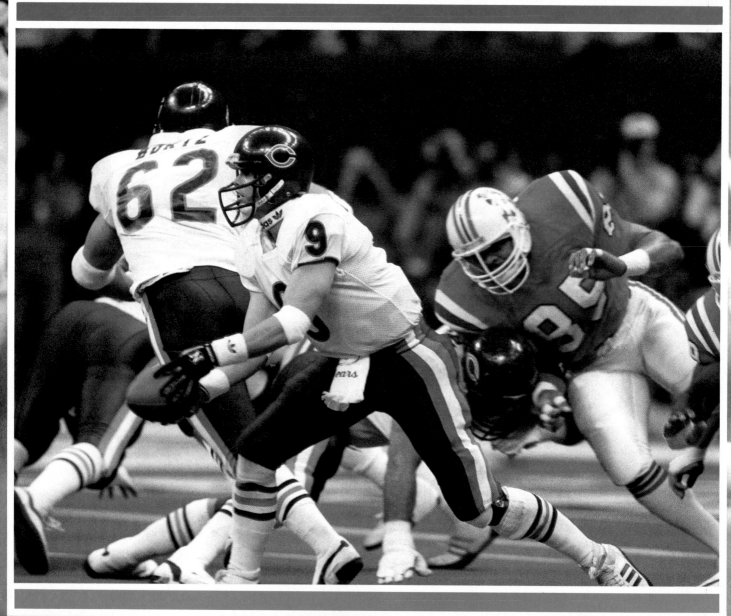

The National Football Conference Championship

Perhaps the Rams should have been tipped off about the Bears temperament earlier in the week. That's when Buddy Ryan, Chicago's outspoken defensive coordinator, told the world that Eric Dickerson, the Rams' All Pro running back, would fumble the ball three times against the aggressive Bears defense. Or perhaps it was the statement made by head coach Mike Ditka who said, "There are teams that are fair-haired, and teams that are not. There are teams named Smith and teams named Grabowski. The Rams are Smith. The Bears are Grabowski."

While the Bears actually don't have anybody named Grabowski, the implications were clear. Ditka all but said that his Bears, the Grabowskis, are blue collar workers, ready to sweat, ready to hit, and ready to get down and dirty. According to Ditka, the Rams, the Smiths, are West Coast beach boys, white collar workers, not ready to mix it up in the frigid atmospheric conditions of frozen Soldier Field.

"My name's been Smith all along, and I never associated it with white collar or conformity," said the Rams' center Doug Smith. "I mean, they're the ones making videos. We could make a video and there would be 50 sales – to our families."

One video they wouldn't buy is the NFC conference championship game, because as the Bears promised, it was a one-sided affair. The final score, 24-0, gave a fair indication of the events. Chicago's defense played another suffocating, brutally physical game. Eric Dickerson failed to live up to the Buddy Ryan expectations, fumbling the ball only twice. And Dieter Brock, the Los Angeles quarterback, was treated like a well garnished main course for 11 hungry Bears.

Brock's longest completion of the day was a 15-yard strike to Tony Hunter. The passing game netted 47 total yards on 10-31. The Bears limited the Rams to 130 total yards for their second straight playoff shutout, an NFL record.

"Two straight shutouts," chortled Bears linebacker Mike Singletary.

Tony Eason and Craig James (previous page) combined to end "The Jinx" for the Patriots while Walter Payton (facing page) shows the form that made him the NFL's all-time leading rusher. Buddy Ryan expected the Rams' Eric Dickerson (above) to fumble three times; Dickerson disappointed, fumbling only twice. Bears' coach Mike Ditka (right) looks on confidently.

"That's not a surprise, it's scary."

"People thought we were too cocky," winning coach Mike Ditka said. "But I don't oppose setting high goals. If you want to do something in life, mark it high on the board."

The Bears, and quarterback Jim McMahon, certainly did. For as outrageous, zany and flaky as McMahon is, that's how good a quarterback he can be. In windblown, snowy Soldier Field, McMahon shot down any critics with a sterling performance, throwing for a touchdown, running for a touchdown and directing an error-free offense. "The wind must not have bothered him too much," Ditka said. "He was our leading rusher (he averaged seven yards per carry), our leading passer (16-25, 166 yards) and he scored as many points (six) as anybody else."

"McMahon was just outstanding," admitted losing coach John Robinson. "He isn't rated high enough. He should get a lot more recognition than he did in the past."

Most of the recognition McMahon gets is for his outlandish behavior. A week before the conference championship, McMahon was fined $5,000 by Commissioner Pete Rozelle for advertising "Adidas" on his headband. So all McMahon did was push the "Adidas" headband to his neck where it's permitted and don a "Rozelle" headband. Even Pete had to smile at that one saying it was "a great gag."

"He was a crazy nut out there," said Bears' running back Walter Payton. "He did everything but take his clothes off, and if we'd been out there longer, he might have done that."

"He was yelling at us to keep our heads out of our butts," said Jim Covert, one of McMahon's offensive linemen. "But that's normal."

So was the way the Bears won the game. McMahon culminated a 5-play, 56-yard first-quarter drive by scampering for a 16-yard touchdown to give the Bears the only points they really needed. Kevin Butler's 34-yard field goal gave the Bears a 10-0 lead after the first half and when McMahon found Willie Gault with a 22-yard TD strike in the third period, the game was a foregone conclusion. To top it off the Bears last score came on a 52-yard fumble recovery by Wilber Marshall.

Score this one for the Grabowskis.

The American Football Conference Championship

Ah, The Jinx. All week as the New England Patriots prepared to battle the Miami Dolphins for the AFC conference championship, all anybody talked about was The Jinx. Forget that New England had won 11 of its last 13 games since a dismal 2-3 start. Forget that the Patriots' forte was running the football, something Miami had trouble contending with. Hanging over the heads of these Patriots was The Jinx.

You could say The Jinx started in 1966, after the Patriots beat the Dolphins 20-14. Since then, The Jinx of the Orange Bowl had struck down the New Englanders regularly. For 18 straight games, the Pats could not beat Miami in the Orange Bowl. That included a 28-13 loss in a 1983 playoff contest and a Monday night game not four weeks past when the Patriots blew a fourth-quarter lead in the final

minute to lose to the Dolphins. Combine The Jinx with the fact that no other wild-card team ever won three straight on the road, that the Dolphins were 5-0 in AFC title games and that Miami had won all nine games at home this season and you could understand why the Pats were the underdogs.

Not only was Dan Marino's passing game (above) stifled by the strong Patriot defense, but so was Tony Nathan (facing page) and the Dolphin rushers. Overleaf: Miami fans felt confident, even though the field conditions (top right) favored New England. Tony Franklin (main picture) boots the Pats to the Super Bowl.

20

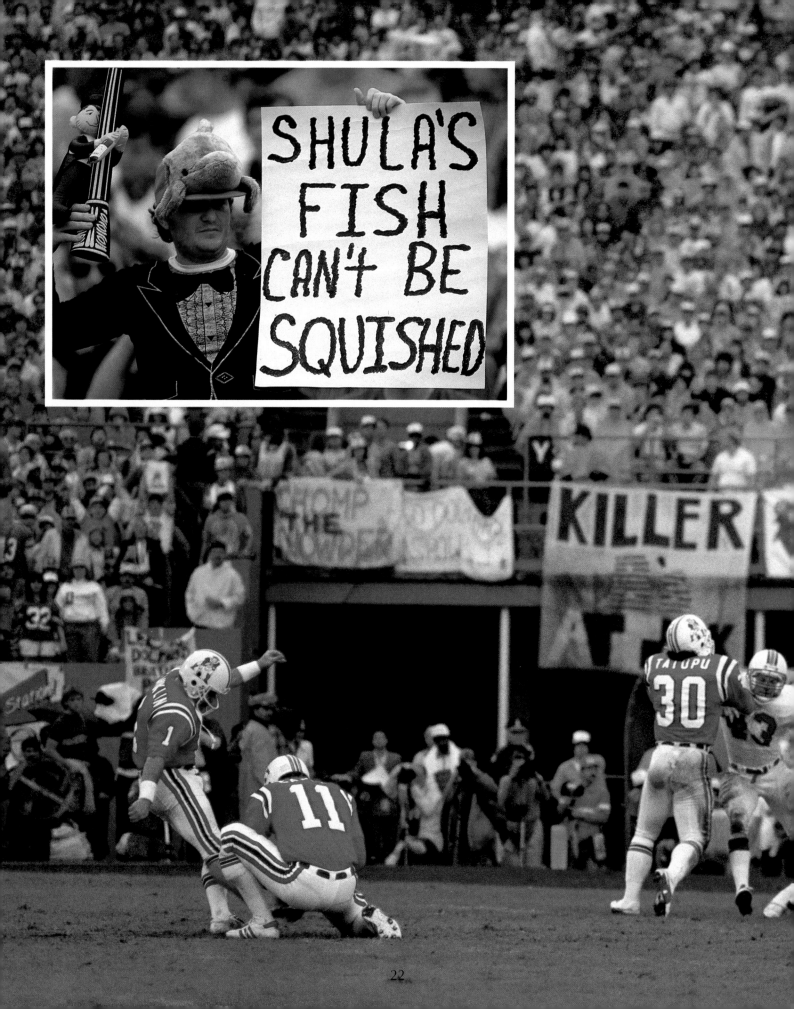

SHULA'S
FISH
CAN'T BE
SQUISHED

KILLER

TATUPU
30

"We ran a lot of bookies out of the business," joked halfback Robert Weathers after New England surprised everyone by crushing the Dolphins 31-14.

"We knew that if we were going to make it to the Super Bowl, we'd have to get there through Miami," commented Patriots guard Ron Wooten. "This is like a dream come true, winning it down here, in this place, against this team."

If it was a dream for the Patriots, it was a nightmare for Miami. The usually mistake-free Dolphins lost four fumbles and Dan Marino was intercepted two times as New England cashed in the mistakes for 24 points.

"It's not a hard game to look at," said a downcast Miami linebacker Jay Brophy. "We made too many mistakes to win. They took advantage of their opportunities and we didn't."

A day-long rain made the playing conditions perfect for the run-oriented Patriots. The soggy, slow Orange Bowl turf was reminiscent of the 1982 AFC title game when the Dolphins running game profited from the conditions to shut out the Jets 14-0. This time it was Miami who were at a disadvantage.

"Rain helped us more," said Patriots' veteran left guard John Hannah. "We're a power-type line. We like to push on 'em."

And push on 'em the Patriots did. New England rushed for 255 yards in 59 carries. The ability to run the football enabled New England to hold the ball twice as long as the Dolphins, serving two purposes. First, it allowed inexperienced quarterback Tony Eason to pick his spots when throwing, as evidenced by his total of 12 passes. Second, it kept Miami's explosive offense, led by Dan Marino, off the field.

"Every time we got into a scoring battle with them, we came out the loser," Wooten said. "With the way our defense is playing, we figured we could hold them to a reasonable number of points. If that happened, we knew we could win."

And they did. The defense played an outstanding game, limiting Marino to 154 yards passing. Marino threw 24 times in the direction of his fleet wide receivers, Mark Duper and Mark

Craig James and the Patriots (facing page) were able to run at will against the porous Dolphin defense, gaining 255 yards on 59 carries. Young Tony Eason (above) displayed a veteran's poise as he quarterbacked the Patriots to a mistake-free offense and a berth against the Big Bad Bears.

Clayton, yet only completed three to each. Patriots' cornerback Raymond Clayborn, an All-Pro, was kept busy all day, batting away six passes.

"There were more passes thrown my way today than in any game in the last two years," said an exhausted Clayborn. "I stayed fresh, though. We came into the game rested. At my age, every little bit of rest during the week helps."

The game's first play from scrimmage was a prelude of things to come for the Dolphins as Tony Nathan fumbled and Garin Veris recovered on the Miami 45. New England moved to the 23-yard line before Tony Franklin kicked the Pats to a 3-0 lead. Miami took its only lead of the day in the second quarter when Bruce Johnson handled a 10-yard pass from Marino to give Miami a 7-3 lead. New England answered immediately with an 8-play, 66-yard drive, culminating in a Tony Eason to Tony Collins four-yard TD.

New England padded its lead with a one-yard pass from Eason to Derrick Ramsey in the second quarter and a two-yard pass to Robert Weathers in the third period. With a 24-7 advantage, the game was all but over. And so was The Jinx.

26

THE ★★TEAMS★★

NFC EAST
DIVISION

New York Giants

Aside from the Super Bowl Champion Chicago Bears, the New York Giants enjoyed the lofty status of being the best defensive team in the NFL. Their attacking 3-4 defense, with arguably the finest crew of linebackers in the league, limited opponents to a mere 3.5 yards per rush, tops in football. Their three-man line, anchored by Leonard Marshall, terrorized opposing quarterbacks, sacking them an NFL high 68 times.

Naturally, when the draft rolls around the Giants, rich in defensive talent, go for defense. In fact, their first six picks (they received four extra selections in last-minute trades of Gary Zimmerman and Mark Haynes) were all defensive players. Eric Dorsey, a 6-5, 280-pound end from Notre

Phil Simms (previous pages left) enjoyed a "Giant" year for New York. The Redskins (previous pages right) prospered even in a transition year. Simms (above) passed the Giants into the playoffs, while little Joe Morris rushed for a team record 1,336 yards. Lawrence Taylor (top right) battled with the Falcons and a substance abuse problem in '85.

Dame, should add depth to the line while a pair of second round picks, cornerback Mark Collins of Cal State-Fullerton and safety Greg Lasker from Arkansas, should help the Giants only question mark, the defensive backfield.

With the defense taken care of, head coach Bill Parcells can concentrate on improving the offense. Phil Simms started that process last year by finally realizing his potential. Part of his problem in the past has been injuries, but in 1985 Simms remained healthy and the offense showed spark. The blond quarterback from Morehead State hit on 55.6 per cent of his passes and threw for 22 touchdowns and 3,829 yards. Simms had help in the backfield as Joe Morris emerged as a legitimate outside threat, becoming a 1,000-yard rusher for the first time.

The major stumbling block for the offense was turnovers. The Giants fumbled the ball 36 times last year, twice as many as the season before, and four passes were picked off and returned for touchdowns.

But these Giants should overcome the mistakes. They have a defense that is comparable to the best and an offense that can strike quickly. Can a championship game with the Bears be far behind?

Washington Redskins

Just like the Los Angeles Raiders, the Washington Redskins underwent football equivalent to surgery last year. Without much warning and without losing too many strides, the Redskins managed to trade in their aging talent for the future and still field a formidable team.

The biggest change was a necessity. The snap of Joe Theismann's leg as Giants' linebacker Lawrence Taylor sacked him on that Monday night, still sends shivers down the spine. It also made little known signalcaller Jay Schroeder a starting quarterback, and the Redskins third-year pro jumped on the opportunity. Schroeder finished his first NFL season of serious playing time by hitting on better than 53 per cent of his passes while calmly directing the Washington offense.

The other significant change was at running back, where George Rogers displaced ancient John Riggins. Riggins, troubled by back problems for years, finally succumbed to the younger man who was obtained from New Orleans prior to the season. Rogers showed his old Heisman Trophy form by rushing for 1,093 yards and seven touchdowns.

All was not new for the Redskins, though. Their defense, always a fine unit, ranked number one against the pass and number three overall.

The Giants' Phil Simms (above left) had plenty of reason to smile last season as he set a plethora of team records at quarterback. Dexter Manley (above) puts the pressure on Atlanta signalcaller David Archer. Facing page: (top) Darrell Green outjumps Dallas' Tony Hill while (bottom) Vernon Dean puts the clamps on a Falcon runner. Overleaf: Simms (top left) was well protected. Big Dave Butz (bottom left and main picture) keep the Skins' reputation as a top defensive team intact. George Rogers (inset bottom right) replaced John Riggins as Washington's leading man.

32

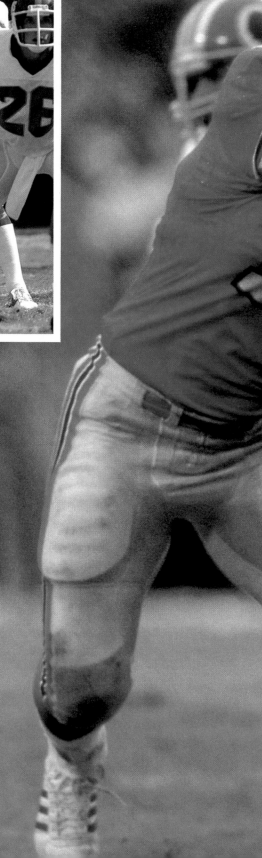

General Manager Bobby Beathard kept his eye on the future, however, when he selected defensive lineman Markus Koch with his first pick. The defensive backfield was buoyed by the unexpected emergence of rookies Raphel Cherry and Barry Wilburn and combined with veterans Darrell Green and Vernon Dean, the Redskins deep four were tough.

And just like the Los Angeles Raiders, you can expect the Redskins to be in the hunt come playoff time.

Dallas Cowboys

Who can ever forget the Hail Mary pass from Roger Staubach to Drew Pearson in the 1975 playoffs that shocked both the Vikings and Cowboys and sent Dallas home a winner. Well, that's the way things used to be for the Cowboys. When they needed a quick score, just send one of the speedy wideouts to the

end zone and, bang!, a touchdown. It doesn't just happen like it used to. And the Cowboys want to change that.

"We've got to have some new people," proclaimed Dallas coach Tom Landry before the NFL draft. "One or two can make a big difference. It could be an explosive wide receiver."

Dallas wanted a speedy wide receiver so bad that it even traded up with the Niners to get him. That him is Mike Sherrard, a standout at UCLA. "I feel extremely good about this pick," Landry said afterwards. "We think Sherrard should be able to start for us this year. He has such great speed (4.4 in the 40-yard dash) and carries it on a 6-2 frame."

The other spot the Cowboys shored up at the draft was running back, where Tony Dorsett has ruled for 10 years. Dorsett, at 32, still gained 1,307 yards, but the Cowboys are

preparing for the future with Darryl Clack, a 5-10, 207 back from Arizona State.

The defense showed some cracks, finished 20th overall and only 26th against the pass in the league. The defensive line ranked fourth in sacks, but three of the starters are over 33 years old. Landry hopes last season's number one selection, Kevin Brooks, can step in and become a force.

The defensive backfield already has a force in cornerback Everson Walls, who led the league in interceptions for the third time last year, the first time anybody has ever done that. Walls picked off nine passes as the Cowboys team total of 34 ranked second in the NFL.

This is a year of transition in Dallas. Their biggest transition may be getting used to not making the playoffs.

Philadelphia Eagles

When Buddy Ryan ran the defensive show for the Chicago Bears his watchword was aggressive. So it comes as no surprise that Ryan's first head coaching job in Philadelphia starts with aggression.

"You don't get anywhere in life if you don't roll the dice," said gambler Buddy Ryan on draft day. "It's just like blitzing on third-and-30. People know we're going to do that, too."

And so on draft day Buddy Ryan rolled the dice. When others said running back Keith Byars may be damaged goods, Buddy Ryan scoffed at it. "Keith can be a franchise player," Ryan said. "I think people who selected ahead of us ran a gut check on the Philadelphia Eagles. We answered it, and I think we're going to answer a bunch of them as the year goes along."

That was not the end of the gamble for Ryan. On the second round, Ryan took Texas A&M fullback

Facing page: Danny White (top) led the Cowboys to another division title with the help of perennial all-pro Randy White (bottom). Eagles' wide receiver Mike Quick (left) looks the ball into his hands.

The running game was led by Earnest Jackson, acquired before the season from San Diego, who became only the third Eagle to gain 1,000 yards rushing in a season. He was not the outside threat Philadelphia needed, so expect Byars to carry much of the load if his injured left foot is healthy.

With Ryan at the helm, the one thing you can expect is changes. And the biggest change may be the Eagles won-loss record.

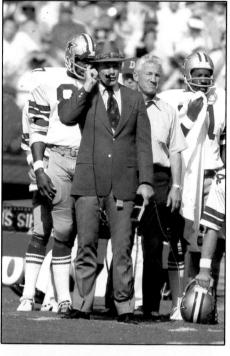

Anthony Toney and a linebacker with a lot of talent and a sorted reputation, Alonzo Johnson of Florida. In the third round, Ryan traded his pick for unproven quarterback Matt Cavanaugh, who will challenge incumbent Ron Jaworski for the starting job. "Nobody automatically becomes number one," Ryan warned after the trade. "We're going to have competition at every position."

That became evident by more off-season moves when Ryan unloaded

The Eagles' world (above) was turned upside down by the Bucs. Tom Landry (top right) manned the sidelines for Dallas while Dexter Manley (bottom) looks on. Crunch! goes the 49ers back (facing page).

three veteran linebackers and cut the starting center. Much of the improvement, though, has to come from the offense, where the Eagles couldn't get out of their own way last year. The offense ranked 15th overall, but a poor 23rd in rushing.

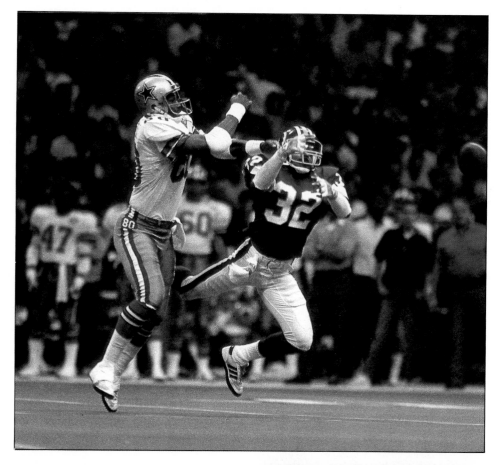

big play to shatter us. "Defensively, I want to be aggressive. We'll blitz and we'll attack.

"If I had to start out right now, we'd start with a 3-4 alignment, primarily because of the personnel we have. We appear to have quality line-backers. Down deep, I'd prefer the 4-3, but I know they played the 4-3 last year and they didn't stop the run or the pass."

Like Stallings said, there is some talent on the defense. Right end Curtis Greer's performance fell off sharply in 1985 as his sack total dropped from 14 to 7. E.J. Junior and second-year man Freddie Joe Nunn are quality linebackers and the draft brought another one, Anthony Bell from Michigan.

St. Louis Cardinals

A strange thing happened to the Cardinals on the way to the Super Bowl. Picked as one of the top contenders for the big prize, the Cardinals found themselves in more trouble than the Bowery Boys. To choose one area which led to St. Louis' miserable 5-11 season would be impossible.

The Cardinals ranked next to last in both sacks made and allowed. The defense intercepted the fewest passes in the league and gave up the most touchdowns. They finished 24th against the rush and the players seemed to give up halfway through the season. Quarterback Neil Lomax ran for his life more times than James Bond and in turn he responded with a horrible season.

But things may change for the better in 1986. The Cards have a new coach, Gene Stallings, with a new attitude and a winning background. "I want us to be a tough football team," says the former Dallas Cowboys assistant. "I want us to be tough mentally and physically. I don't want a

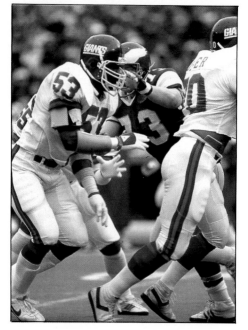

Dallas and Washington fought all season (top). Harry Carson (above) anchored the Giants linebackers that gave Neil Lomax (above right) of the Cardinals fits. Facing page: fans and cheerleaders (top) made their feelings known, while the St. Louis defense (bottom) does the same to a New Orleans back.

The offensive line needs to be retooled to give Lomax time to spot wide receiver Roy Green, who was hobbled by injuries all season and never approached the all pro status of previous years. The backfield is in the capable hands of Ottis Anderson and Stump Mitchell and the kicking game should get a kick out of draftee John Lee, the top placekicker in college football a year ago.

Still, there are too many question marks to think the Cards will reach the plateau they were so near.

LONGNECKS &
SKINSBUSTERS
NOWHERE BUT
"TEXAS"

NFC CENTRAL DIVISION

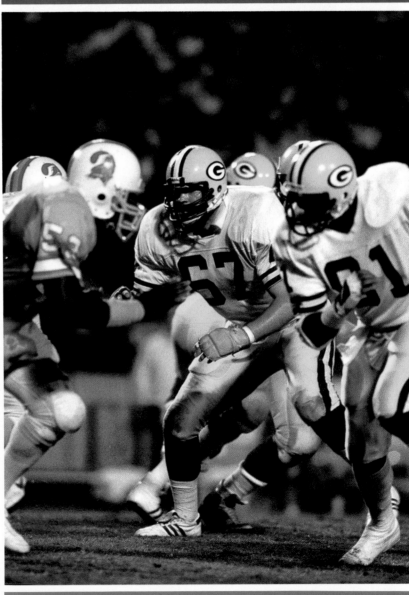

Chicago Bears

What can you say about a team that won 15 of 16 regular season games, that didn't allow a point in two playoff games, and destroyed a good team in the Super Bowl? How about it's not going to be as easy to repeat this season.

Sure the Bears are the odds-on favorites to win another NFL Championship but, after the 1985

season, many things have changed. The most important change is in the coaching staff. Head coach Mike Ditka is still there, but Buddy Ryan, the outspoken defensive coordinator and creator of the "46" defense, has left to coach Philadelphia. Ryan took two assistants with him and Ditka faces a challenge of rebuilding his surrounding staff.

"I think any time you lose coaches of the quality we lost, you have to be concerned," says Ditka. "I have a great deal of confidence in the people we've hired who are just as capable, but it will take time for everyone to familiarize themselves with each other. It will take an adjustment period for our players to get confidence in the new coaches and what they are going to try to accomplish."

What they'll try to accomplish is a repeat of last season, which saw the Bears finish first in overall defense for the second consecutive season,

linebackers in the league and Gary Fencik anchors the defensive backfield which lost starting right cornerback Leslie Frazier to a knee injury in the Super Bowl.

The offense reached a crescendo as Jim McMahon emerged not only as a severe flake, but as a premier quarterback in the league. Walter Payton is a year older, but "Sweetness" didn't show any signs of slowing down and the offensive line, headed by All-Pro Jim Covert, gives McMahon and company plenty of time to operate.

If you're expecting the Bears to get fat on their Super season, don't.

allowing only 258 yards per game. And the Bear defense is just reaching its peak. Richard Dent culminated a remarkable year at defensive end by winning the Super Bowl MVP. Mike Singletary heads up the finest group of

Richard Dent (above left) was the Super Bowl MVP of a swarming Bears defense (above) which led the league. Steve Fuller (facing page) is sacked by an ornery Redskin. James Wilder (previous page main picture) led the Bucs attack.

44

Because when it's time for kickoff, the Bears will be ready to defend their title.

Tampa Bay Buccaneers

The Tampa Bay Bucs could have been the most improved team in the league merely on the strength of their draft. Bo Jackson, the most highly touted running back to come out of college since Earl Campbell, is a mixture of blazing speed and brute strength. Teamed with James Wilder, the most underrated back in the league, Tampa's offense could open up and instead of losing those close contests, the Bucs could have put a few in the "W" column. But Bo chose to play baseball instead of football, thus leaving Tampa in the same situation as last season.

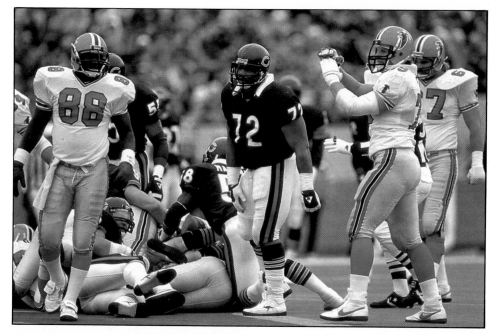

The Falcons signal for timeout as William Perry and the Bears (top) swarm. Bo Jackson (left) chose baseball instead of teaming with James Wilder (above) in the Bucs backfield. The Rams and Bucs (facing page) get to know each other better.

Even before the draft, Bucs coach Leeman Bennett acknowledged the need for a diversified offense. "We had a workmanlike offense last year and I feel we need to acquire players who will give us more weapons, more explosiveness. We will be looking to find more backs to take some of the load off of James (Wilder) and to diversify our offense with more two-back alignments."

Another offensive need came via the trade route when perennial all-pro Marvin Powell was acquired from the Jets to shore up the right tackle spot. The only other question on offense is quarterback Steve Young. The former Brigham Young star and USFL refugee was signed the second week of the season and started the team's final five games. Young hit on better than 50 per cent of his passes, but sometimes he seemed more interested in scrambling (233 yards) than passing.

The defense was a mess last year, finishing 26th overall, but the addition of defensive genius Jim Stanley, the former Michigan Panther coach, plus a heavy emphasis on defense in the

47

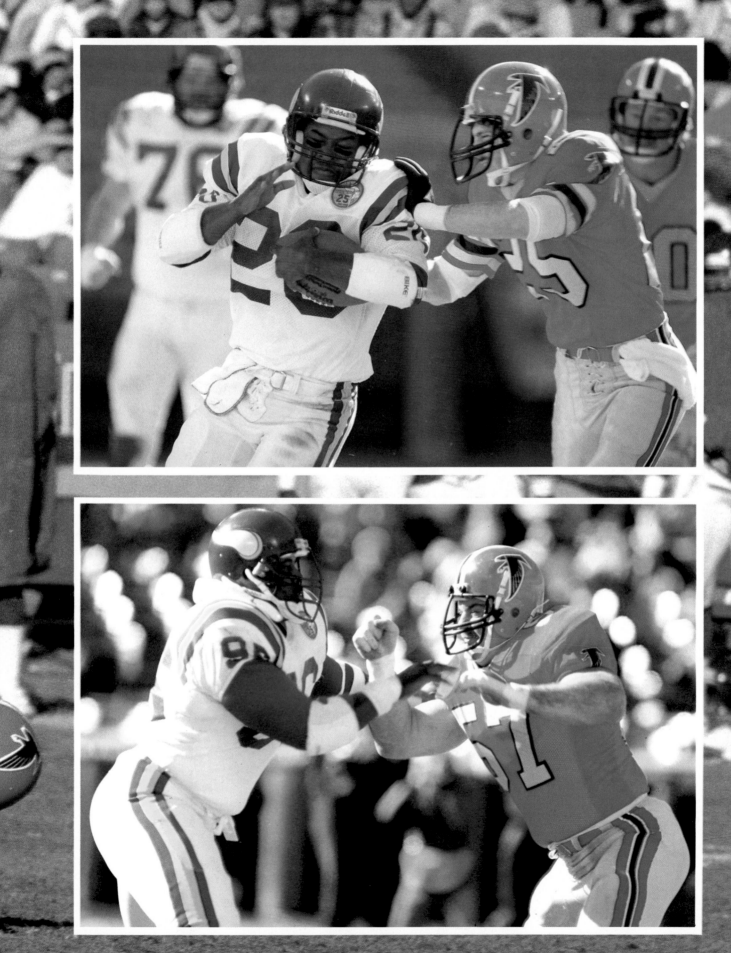

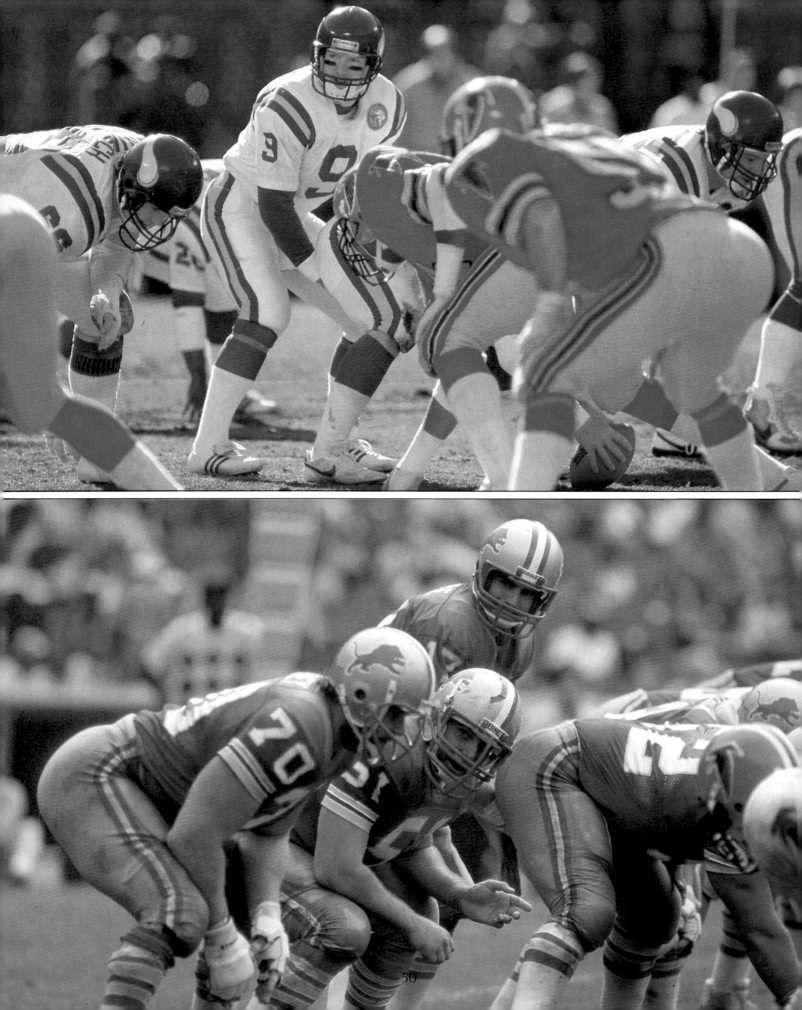

draft, should straighten out that problem.

Now the only problem for Tampa Bay is putting all the pieces together.

Minnesota Vikings

New Minnesota head coach Jerry Burns is realistic when evaluating his Vikings chances in 1986. "We're not in the category yet where we are recognized as legitimate contenders or recognized as a legitimate playoff team. But I think that we are close enough that if we get some development from our younger players and improvement from our veteran players, we can be a contending team."

The Minnesota Vikings and Atlanta Falcons (previous pages) show the strains of playing football. Facing page: (top) Tommy Kramer shouts the signals for Minnesota while Eric Hipple (bottom and below) does the same for Detroit. Greg Coleman (right) took care of the punting duties for the Vikes and Darrin Nelson (below right) handled the running chores.

The one area that needs dramatic improvement is the offensive line, which yielded 45 sacks to the opposition despite having Tommy Kramer, a fine scrambler, at quarterback. Kramer's need to scramble certainly put a damper on his performance as the 10-year veteran threw 26 interceptions last year. But reinforcement is here, now that Gary Zimmerman has taken his game from the courts to the field. With the legal problems for the USFL refugee behind him, Zimmerman is a fine addition to the line.

"I was pleased that we were able to trade for the rights to Gary Zimmerman because he is a seasoned pro," Burns said. "I always say it takes a minimum of three years to play the offensive line at this level, but Zimmerman has already made the transition to professional football."

With improved protection, Kramer will be able to exploit the teams strength, its wide receivers. Anthony Carter, Leo Lewis, Mike Jones and Buster Rhymes gives the

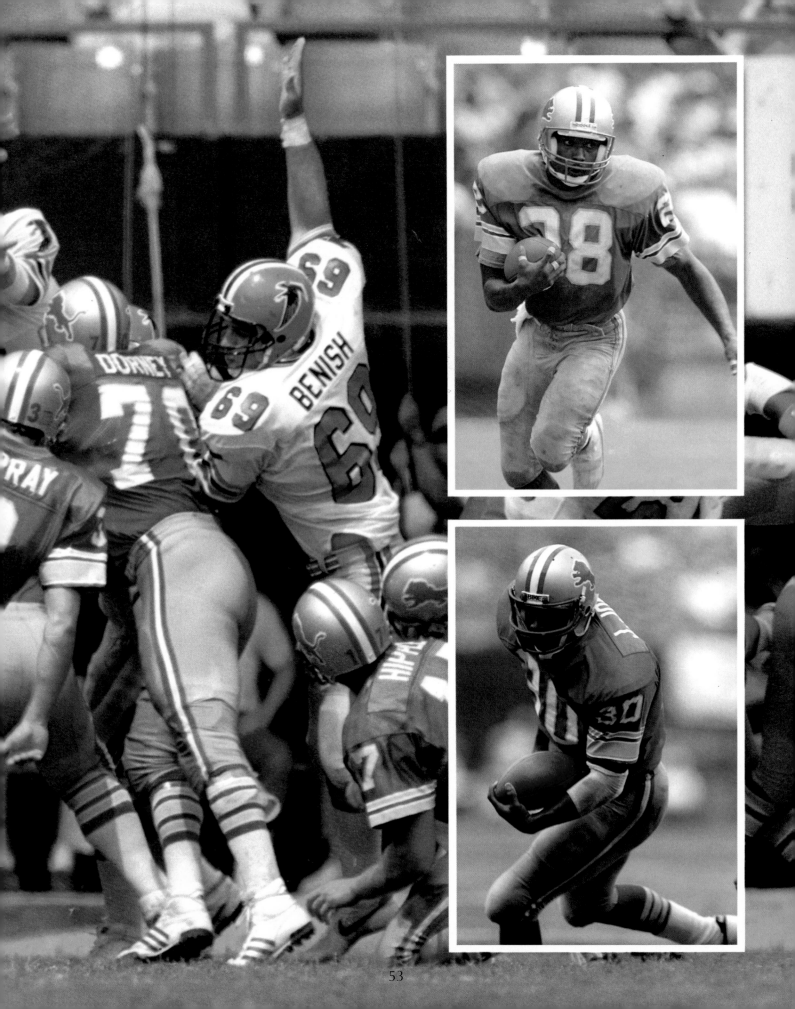

Vikes both depth and talent at the receiver position.

The defense should also come around, now that Floyd Peters is the new coordinator and he has number one draft pick, Gerald Robinson, a pass rushing demon, on his side.

If all cylinders click for the Vikes, look for them to make the playoffs as a wild card team.

Detroit Lions

Will the real Detroit Lions please stand up. Is it the Lions squad which roared to a 6-2 record at home, beating such notables as Dallas, San Francisco, Miami and the Jets? Or is it the 1-7 road team which lost to pushover Tampa Bay and Indianapolis? The answer probably lies somewhere in between.

The Lions are the quintessential .500 team, needing a few players on both sides of the line to make any drastic improvement. Detroit finished as the 28th ranked team in total offense last season and the offense took no solace from the fact that one-time star running back, Billy Sims, formally announced his retirement due to knee problems. But the Lions may have patched their wound in the draft when Garry James surprisingly was available in the second round. The 5-10, 204-pound back from LSU has been clocked in 4.49 for the 40 and his blazing speed is just what the Lions outside game needs. "His speed certainly fits what we needed for our backfield," said coach Darryl Rogers. "Garry was one of the fastest running backs on the board and I think he'll develop into a very fine pro back."

The Lions first pick is also expected to be a fine pro, but quarterback Chuck Long will not be rushed into the lineup. Instead, Long will be gaining experience on the sidelines behind starter Eric Hipple. Hipple is coming off his best year statistically, completing 55 per cent of his passes and throwing 17 TDs.

The offense was not the only unit which lost a key player to retirement. Doug English, a veteran lineman, called it quits after suffering a neck fracture and Keith Ferguson will be counted on to replace English. The Lions defense yielded the most yards on the ground in the league with the

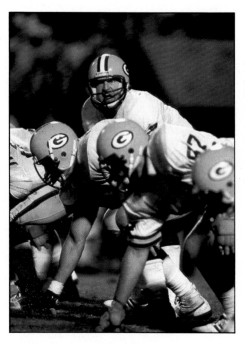

exception of Houston and the leading tackler was a safety. That should give you an indication of the shape the Lions are in.

A .500 season would be a positive step for these Lions.

Green Bay Packers

The question facing Green Bay head coach Forrest Gregg this season is this: does he force feed Robbie Bosco, the third round selection from Brigham Young, who as a hot shot collegian broke many of the records held by Steve Young and Jim McMahon. Or does Gregg play it safe with veterans Lynn Dickey, Vine Ferragamo or Randy Wright?

"We have four people there that we all know can play," Gregg said. "But, at the same time, we don't know who that number one guy's going to be right now."

Gregg should just be lucky that Bosco was around when the Packers selected in the third round. The elusive Bosco is rebounding from a shoulder injury which left teams wary, but then again the same questions surrounded Joe Montana when he was drafted by San Francisco in 1979.

Quarterback was a major problem for the 8-8 Packers last season as Lynn Dickey fought through two pre-season injuries, a slow start and an offensive line that couldn't give him adequate time to spot his

Eddie Murray (previous pages main picture) boots one for the Lions. Detroit had no trouble running the ball at home, but on the road (insets) the results weren't nearly as good. Lynn Dickey (above left and facing page bottom left) suffered through an injury-plagued season. The Packers' running game (above and facing page bottom right) were below par, as was the passing game (facing page top).

receivers. With the gimpy-kneed Dickey and a line that had four of the five starting linemen new starters since 1983, Green Bay QBs were sacked 50 times a year ago. Things should improve drastically in 1986 as this unit of young veterans gels into a fine line.

Whoever the quarterback turns out to be, he'll be fortunate to have two outstanding receivers in all-pro James Lofton and tight end Paul Coffman. The running back trio of Eddie Lee Ivery, Jessie Clark and Gerry Ellis combine for a fine unit although they do lack the one standout.

Gregg has steadily made the defense into a stellar outfit in his tenure as Green Bay coach. In the past three seasons, the defense has gone from 28th and last in the league in 1983 to 16th in '84 and 12th last year. Improvement will continue as expected.

But until the Pack gets the quarterback situation straightened out, Green Bay is destined for the cellar in the Central Division.

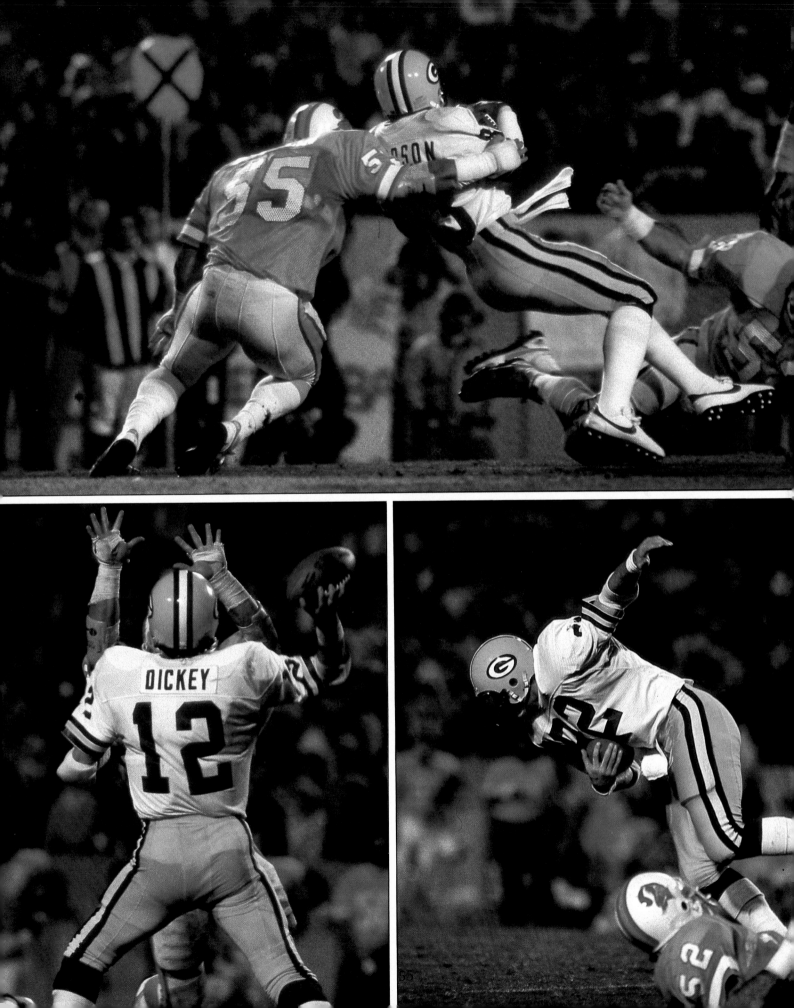

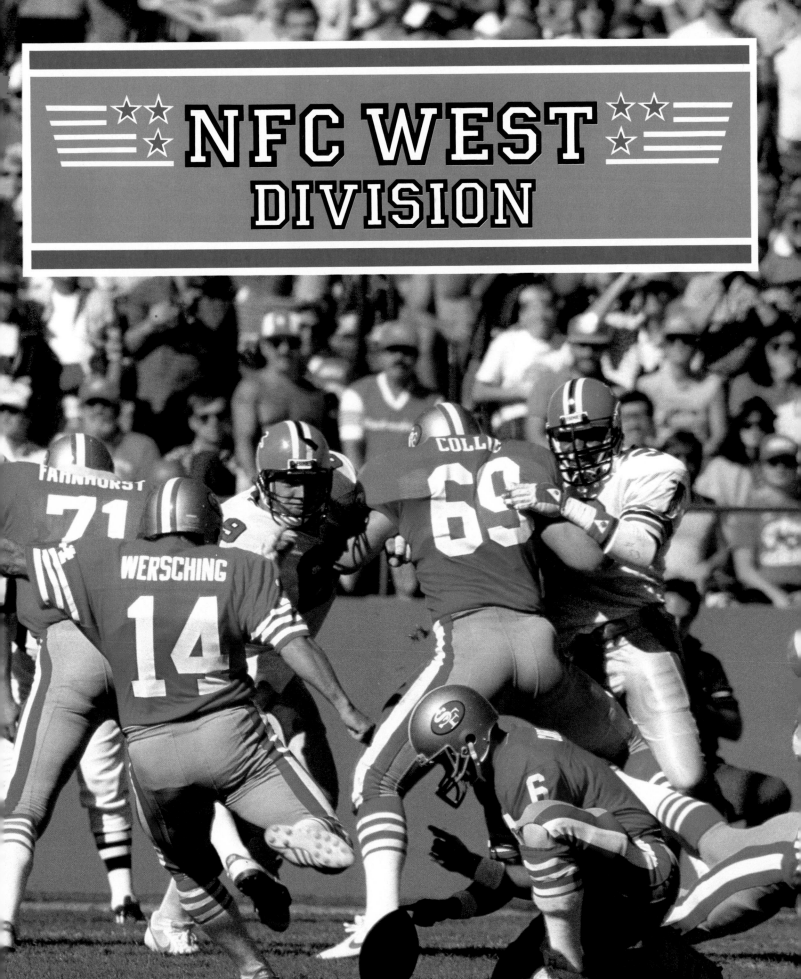

NFC WEST
DIVISION

Los Angeles Rams

Each year of John Robinson's reign as head coach of the Rams, Los Angeles has improved. In 1983, Robinson stepped into a bad situation and turned the team around, leading them to nine victories and a playoff spot. A year later, the Rams built on that foundation with a 10 win season and another spot in post season play. But in 1985, the Rams put everything together, winning the NFC West and going on to the conference championship before falling to the eventual Super Bowl Champs.

Now that Los Angeles has reached the lofty heights of the NFL's elite, Robinson will fine tune the team, trying to attain that next plateau.

The area which could use the most fine tuning is the offensive line, which has seen age creep up like a blitzing linebacker. Three of the starters are older than 30 and still four of the starting five made All-Pro. Despite that status, quarterback Dieter Brock was sacked 57 times and Robinson realizes the offensive line needs to be retooled.

"We must make an overall improvement this year, in both the running and the passing game," Robinson admitted. "The first place to look for that is in the offensive line."

To help expedite the process, Robinson used his first two draft picks on linemen, selecting Mike Schad and Tom Newberry. Robinson is especially high on Schad. "Physically, he's the best line prospect any of us have ever seen," he said about the 6-5, 290-pound tackle who starred in Canada at Queens College. "I've had great players like Anthony Munoz (at USC) and this man has some similar attributes. He's very intelligent and very competitive."

Brock, another Canadian, had a rough year in his first season in the NFL. The former Canadian Football League star connected on almost 60 per cent of his passes, yet the Rams finished last in passing offense. Eric Dickerson, the record breaking running back of 1984 started slowly after a training camp holdout, but still managed well over 1,000 yards.

The defense was the Rams strength all season as the line dramatically improved its play

compared to 1984. The most striking area was in the pass rush with veteran Gary Jeter registering a team-high 11 quarterback sacks.

With Robinson at the helm , Dickerson in camp from the outset

and an improved offensive line, the Rams may meet the Bears again for the conference championship.

New Orleans Saints

The New Orleans Saints will start all over again, and new owner Tom Benson has hired just the man to do it. Jim Finks, who gave the Chicago Bears the foundation that reaped the benefits last season, will take over the general manager duties. As his first coach, Finks hired former USFL head coach Jim Mora, who led the Baltimore/Philadelphia Stars to two championships.

The task, though, will not be an easy one. The Saints offense ranked next to last overall and 24th in passing. Bobby Hebert, a star in the USFL, will get a full shot this season after starting six games last year. While his stats weren't gaudy, Hebert did move the team considerably better than either Richard Todd or Dave Wilson.

Hebert better be on his game because the Saints running attack produced only four touchdowns, far and away the worst total in the league. Finks took the first step in improving that situation by drafting massive Jim Dombrowski, a 6-5, 289-pound tackle from Virginia with his top pick. Dombrowski should help open holes for a pair of rookie running backs, Dalton Hilliard, the Saints second pick, and Rueben Mayes, the third selection.

The defense is almost as bad as the offense. The Saints ranked 24th overall and the pass defense allowed almost 57 per cent of the opposition passes to be completed. There are some good, young players, like three-time Pro Bowl linebacker Rickey Jackson and second-year pro Jack Del Rio, but the defense still needs work.

At least now the Saints are heading in the right direction.

Ray Wersching and the Niners (previous pages) weren't locks anymore, whether it was kicking field goals or winning the division. Barry Redden (top) filled in when Eric Dickerson held out. David Archer (above left) was one of three quarterbacks used by the Saints, while Dieter Brock (facing page) guided the Rams. Los Angeles (overleaf) battled the Falcons (top) and the Bucs (main picture) en route to winning the West.

SAINTS ALIVE!

San Francisco 49ers

There's no question that the San Francisco 49ers have some of the best talent in the league. They have the league's best quarterback, Joe Montana, the league's best all-around running back, Roger Craig, and one of the best wide receivers, Dwight Clark. The offense is not much of a problem. The defense, though, is another story.

A check at the stats reveals that San Francisco finished a dismal 14th overall on defense and only 21st in defending the pass. Sure you could blame it on the influx of four new starters, nose tackle Michael Carter, linebackers Todd Shell and Michael Walter and end John Harty. The only problem with that is those four were some of the more productive players on the defense. In fact, Michael Carter emerged as one of the best at his

position in the league. When Carter was injured, the Niners record was 3-4.

"Mike (Carter) is considered the outstanding nose tackle in the NFL," coach Bill Walsh states matter-of-factly. "He is explosive, powerful and quick. He has a dramatic impact on the game while in the lineup."

Explosiveness and quickness were missing from the line most of the season as sack totals dipped like Johnson and Johnson stock. And in the NFL, if you don't have a ferocious pass rush, forget the big time.

The big time says it all for Joe Montana, who enjoyed another fine

Roger Craig and Joe Montana (below left and right) were the 49ers main offensive weapons. Facing page: San Fran's line play (top) needed help, while mistakes (bottom) were costly. Overleaf: the Saints' offense (insets) was sporadic. Main Picture: Dwight Clark.

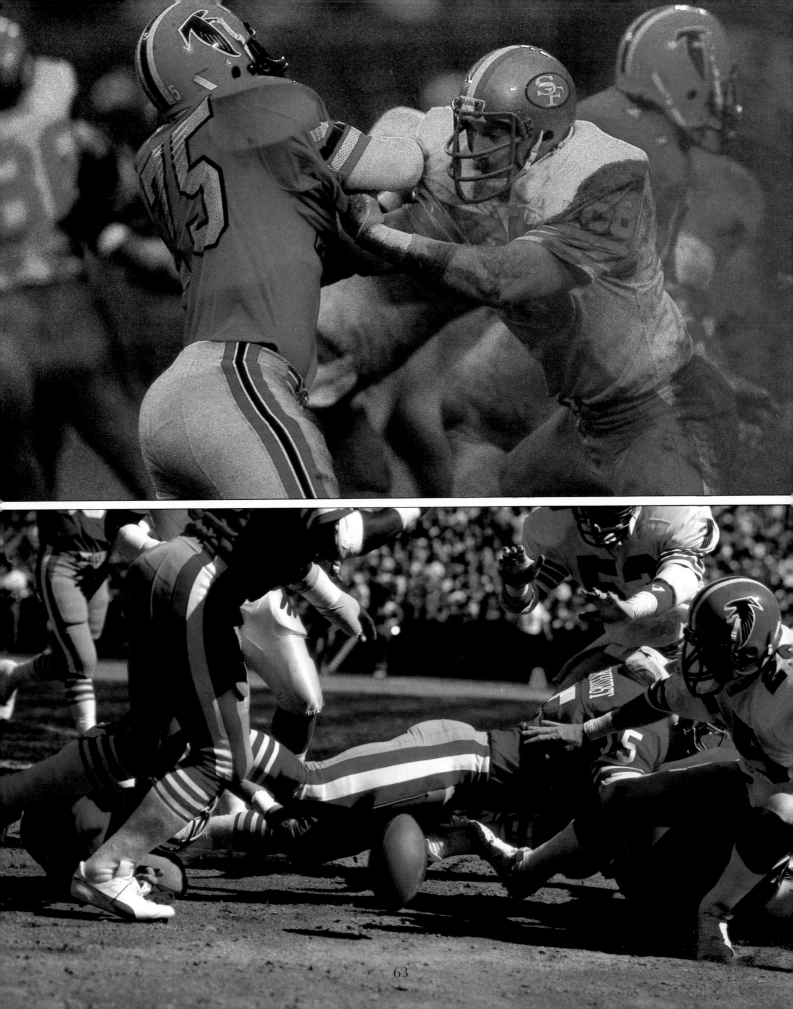

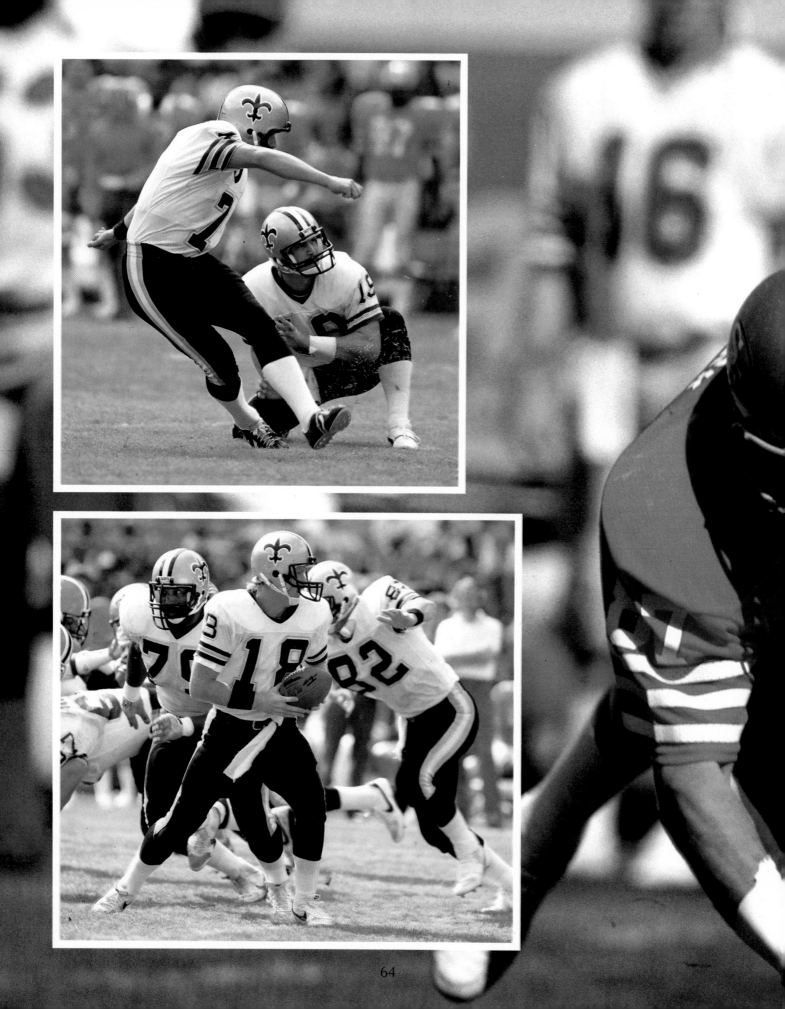

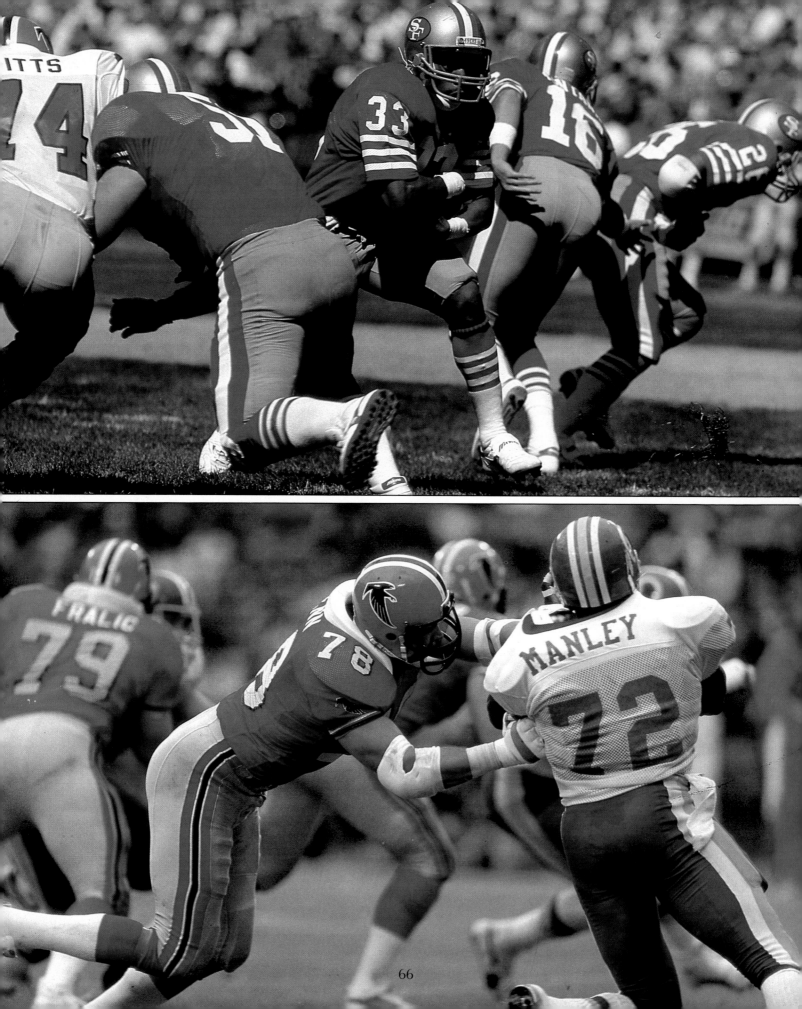

Atlanta Falcons

The Atlanta Falcons know that success in the NFL comes with a strong defense. And the Falcons know that the one thing they didn't possess in 1985 was even an adequate defense. In this case, the statistics don't lie.

Atlanta allowed 452 points, the most in the league. They gave up 32 touchdowns and 4129 yards passing, both the next-to-worst marks in the NFL. Nineteen of their 56 touchdowns allowed on the defense were for 20 yards or more. Talk about giving up the big play.

But the Falcons have a plan to revamp the defense. Start with new defensive coordinator Marion Campbell and continue with an outstanding draft. With the second overall selection, Atlanta jumped on monstrous nose tackle Tony Casillas from Oklahoma. Combined with former first rounders Mike Pitts and Rick Bryan, the Falcons will rush the

Facing page: Roger Craig (top) set an NFL record by rushing and receiving for more than 1,000 yards each. Atlanta's Mike Kenn (bottom) fights off Dexter Manley. Gerald Riggs (top) was the bright spot for the Falcons as their braintrust (above) plots strategy at the draft. Overleaf: the typical scenes at a football game: an injury, plenty of fans and lovely cheerleaders.

season with the Niners. Montana had the best quarterback rating (91.3) in the conference, throwing for 3,653 yards and 27 touchdowns and garnered another selection to the Pro Bowl. He was joined in the backfield by record-setting runner/receiver Roger Craig. All Craig accomplished in 1985 was becoming the first player in league history to surpass 1,000 in both rushing and receiving in the same season.

But, as the 49ers learned last year, you can't live on offense alone.

quarterback with abandon in 1986. With Casillas and the other first-round rookie, linebacker Tim Green from Syracuse, you know why the folks down south are jubilant about the draft.

The offense is not much better than the "D". Falcon quarterbacks were sacked an astonishing 69 times. No wonder Steve Bartkowski and his

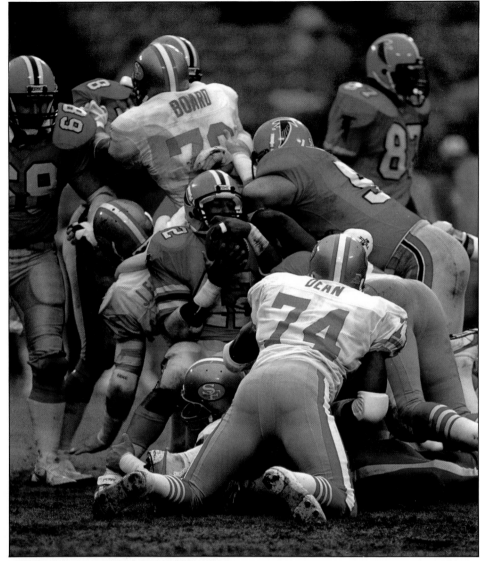

Gerald Riggs (facing page and right) proved to be a workhorse for the Falcons as he lead the NFL in carries attempts and finished second to Marcus Allen of the Los Angeles Raiders in rushing with, 1,719 yards. Mick Luckhurst (bottom and below) did the placekicking for the Falcons.

bum knees were forced to move west behind the relative security of the Los Angeles Rams line. David Archer took the brunt of the line's problems and even hit on 51.6 per cent of his passes. His ratio of touchdown passes to interceptions (7-17), though, left coach Dan Henning an unhappy man.

Those poor pass protectors sure could pave a way for a runner, though, as Gerald Riggs became a workhorse in the backfield. Riggs led the conference in rushing with 1,719 yards, 40 less than NFL rushing champion Marcus Allen. Riggs managed to carry the ball nearly 400 times, score 10 touchdowns and still remain in virtual anonymity. Maybe some day they'll realize this guy's a star.

The Falcons better hope so because they don't have much else right now.

AFC EAST DIVISION

Miami Dolphins

When the talk turns to the Miami Dolphins, the talk usually turns to their head coach Don Shula. And the one word synonymous with Don Shula is winner. For the 12th time in the last 16 seasons, Shula took the Miami Dolphins to the top of the AFC East Division. Last season may have been the most magical yet, as far as coaching goes, for the 56-year-old Shula.

The Dolphins stumbled out of the blocks, were 5-4 after nine games and then, like magic, the Dolphs beat everyone they should and everyone they shouldn't, like the Bears. But even though Miami finished with an 11-5 record, Shula has many holes to fill.

The most obvious weakness on the Dolphins is run defense. That was best highlighted during the playoffs when Cleveland ran through the

middle of the Dolphin defense like it was the center of a doughnut. The Dolphins were lucky to beat Cleveland that day, but the thought has remained indelibly in the mind of Shula. "When I look back on last season," he says, "all I can think of is how lucky we were to get by Cleveland. Most of the time our run defense was just trying to be average."

It was not only during the playoffs that Miami's run defense looked like it was on vacation. During the regular season, Miami ranked 23rd in run defense and 23rd overall. Even the pass "D" collapsed, ranking 22nd in the league.

The Dolphins and the Bills (previous pages) are at the top and bottom of the East, respectively. Doug Betters (left) and Mack Moore (below) give the Miami fans (bottom left) reasons to cheer. Mark Clayton (facing page) spikes the ball for the Dolphins.

New York Jets

Give credit to Joe Walton. After 1984's abysmal season, the Jets head coach had every reason to panic when New York got blown away 31-0 in the season opener against the Raiders. Worse than that, his hand-picked quarterback, Ken O'Brien, was sacked 11 times and looked shakier than a tightrope walker.

But Walton stuck with O'Brien and third-year signalcaller came through with a banner season as the Jets finished 11-5 and in the playoffs for the first time since 1982.

Fuad Reveiz (above and facing page top) gave the Dolphins a reason to kick as he was near the top of the league in field goal accuracy. The Miami offensive line tries to pave a path for running back Lorenzo Hampton (facing page bottom) while the Buffalo defense tries to defend.

But this season Shula will have Hugh Green (acquired from Tampa Bay during the season) and Bob Brudzinski (training camp holdout) from the start.

The offense has no such problems as Dan Marino shook off a training camp holdout to give Miami the second-best passing attack in the league. This despite missing star wide receiver Mark Duper for seven games with an injury.

With Shula ready to work on the defense, Miami should repeat as division champions.

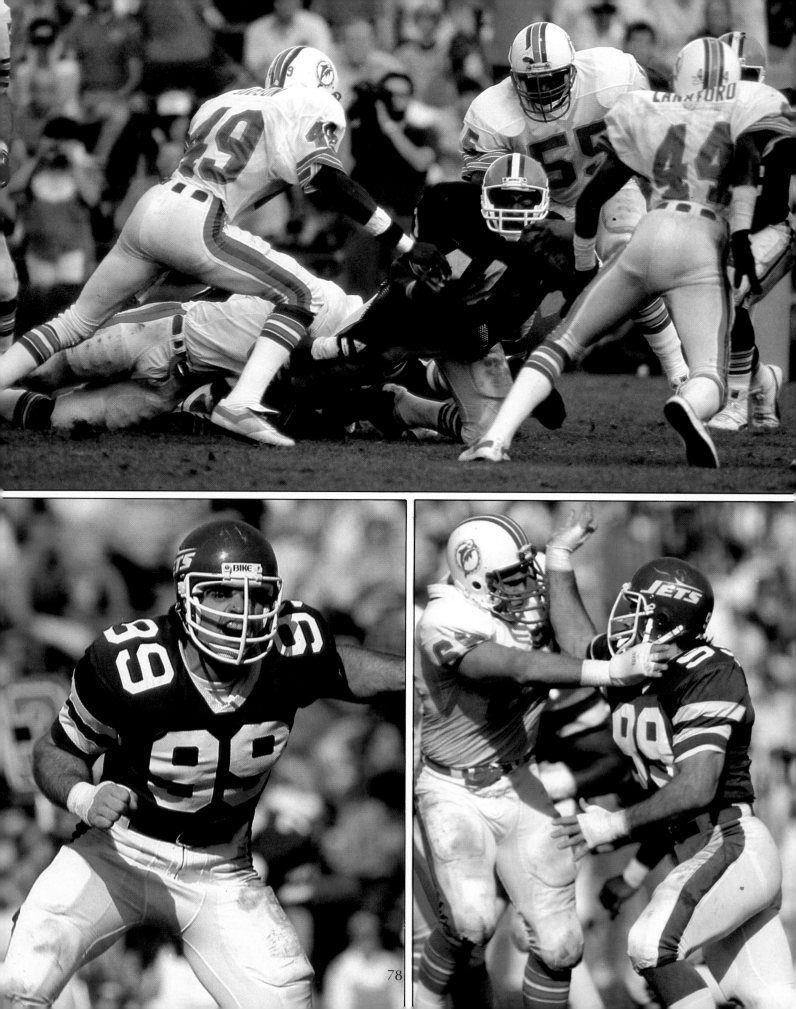

O'Brien came to the fore mixing his pinpoint passing with a strong rushing attack as the Jets offense bolted to number four in the league. O'Brien himself led the NFL in quarterback ratings with a 96.2 and his ratio of touchdown passes to interceptions (25-8) was the best in the league. The only negative was that O'Brien was sacked 62 times, most in the conference.

But the Jets feel they've taken care of that. New York shook up the offensive line by trading perennial all-pro tackle Marvin Powell to Tampa Bay and drafting two behemoth tackles on the first two rounds. Mike Haight, from Iowa, was a surprise pick in the first round and Doug Williams, a highly regarded lineman from Texas A&M, should shore up the weakness.

The Jets defense had no such weakness under the tutelage of Bud Carson. Carson instituted the 3-4 defense and the Jets responded with the eighth best defense in the league.

The only thing missing, besides the health of the defensive backfield, was a rushing linebacker, and the Jets hope third pick Tim Crawford, will fill that void.

For the first time in a while, though, the Jets weaknesses don't outnumber their strengths.

New England Patriots

Not many people could have anticipated New England's rise to the top of the AFC. After all, this was a franchise that had never won an NFL playoff game before last season. A

The Miami defense gang-tackles Cleveland's Earnest Byner (facing page top). Mark Gastineau shows the intensity of the game (facing page bottom left) before he battles a Dolphin offensive lineman (facing page bottom right). Marty Lyons (left) was an important cog in the Jets' defense. Woody Bennett (below) proved to be an important part of the Dolphins attack.

year ago, they were unknown. This season, everyone knows them. And everyone will be gunning for them.

"In the 1986 season," says Patriots' coach Raymond Berry, "we'll be facing a challenge we've never faced before – the challenge of teams liking nothing more than to knock off a Super Bowl team. In order to meet this challenge, it's going to take an attitude that's extremely hardnosed and

Facing page: New England's offensive line takes a breather on the sidelines before blocking for 1,000-yard rusher Craig James (bottom). Wide receiver Irving Fryar (right) and quarterback Steve Grogan (far right) hooked up many times before Grogan injured a knee against the Jets. Below: the Dolphins and the Bills (below) fight it out on the line of scrimmage.

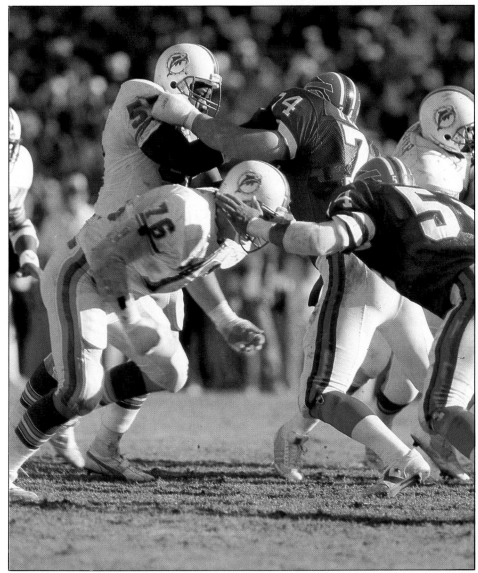

extremely determined to become the best. It's going to take everything we've got to do that. I believe this team will do it."

Maybe, maybe not. Last season everything fell into place perfectly. Steve Grogan goes down with an injury against the Jets and Tony Eason, an erratic quarterback since he was drafted in 1983, runs the offense like a veteran.

He did have some help, though. Craig James spearheaded the sixth best rushing attack in the league and combined with a super offensive line, Eason was able to pick his spots to throw.

The defense, anchored by all-world linebacker Andre Tippett, swarmed opposing offenses, leading to 128 points scored by the offense after turnovers. Tippett finished second for the second consecutive season in sacks with 16 and safety Fred Marion ranked near the top of the league with seven interceptions.

Still, with everybody looking for them, don't look for the Pats to repeat their 1985 miracle.

Indianapolis Colts

If only the Colts had a passing game. That was the feeling coach Rod Dowhower had following another dismal 5-11 season in Indianapolis. All the other pieces for a winning team seemed to be there.

The Colts have built one of the better defenses in the league led by a super linebacking corp of Johnie Cooks, Duane Bickett, Barry Krauss and Cliff Odom. The only weakness was in sacks, but the Colts have taken care of that with their first draft pick (fourth overall) Jon Hand, a great pass rusher from Alabama.

The running game was the envy of many teams around the league as the Colts finished fifth overall rushing the pigskin. The offensive line cut down quarterback sacks from 58 in 1984 to 35 last season and things will only get

better for this young unit.

Even the passing game may come around in 1986. Gary Hogeboom, he of the immense potential, came over in a trade from Dallas prior to the draft. He's never produced in a big way when the Cowboys called on him, yet always complained of a lack of playing time. The Colts quarterback job is his. Now it's up to Hogeboom to stop talking and start producing.

And if he does produce, the AFC East may have a new power.

Chris Hinton of the Colts (below left) developed into one of the league's finest offensive linemen, while the young Indianapolis defense (facing page) made the opposition pay for yardage. The Bills stumbled all season (left) behind QB Bruce Mathiason. Below: Miami's Dwight Stephenson and Buffalo's Fred Smerlas battle on the line.

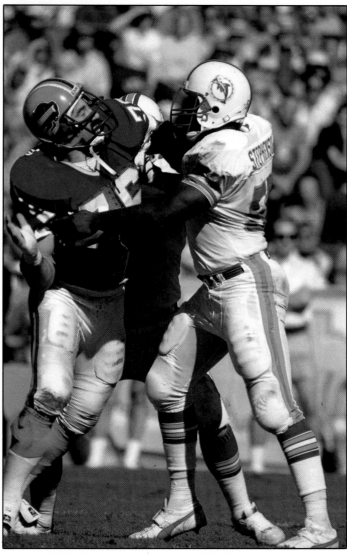

Buffalo Bills

What can you say about a team that's gone 2-14 the past two years, that ranked 28th (that's last folks) in the league in turnover ratio and that's been rumored to be moving to Phoenix?

"There's a lot of work to be done," understates Bills' coach Hank Bullough, who took over the club after four games last year. "There isn't a single area of our team which couldn't be upgraded."

Let's start with the offense, or lack thereof. The Bills finished 25th overall, combining a poor running game with a lousy passing attack. Quarterback

Bruce Mathison took over from Vince Ferragamo during the season and, except for Ferragamo, finished dead last in the quarterback ratings in the NFL. His ratio of interceptions to touchdown passes (14-4) left the people of Buffalo hoping for a blizzard so he would have to hand off the ball instead of throw it.

The rushing game was also a disappointment, but that was mainly due to an offensive line that couldn't move a pee-wee team. The Bills shored that up in the draft, though, acquiring tackle Will Wohlford from Vanderbilt with the 20th overall selection and center Leonard Burton

Buffalo's second-year running back sensation Greg Bell and Miami's outstanding linebacker Bob Brudzinski (facing page) collide head-on in a game at the Orange Bowl. The Bills may have won this battle vs. the Dolphins (above), but they lost the war.

from South Carolina in the third round.

The defense was only slightly better than the offense, placing 17th overall. The major concern was on the line, where the Bills' 25 sacks was the worst in the league.

There should be some improvement in Buffalo in 1986. Just don't expect a lot.

AFC CENTRAL DIVISION

Cleveland Browns

"By bringing in Lindy (Infante), we've made a statement about improving our passing game." Those are the words of head coach Marty Schottenheimer, whose first full season as coach of the Browns resulted in an 8-8 mark and a Central Division championship.

With a new, innovative offensive coordinator like Lindy Infante, Schottenheimer is addressing the Browns' biggest weakness, the passing game. Even with heralded first

round pick Bernie Kosar, the Browns finished 25th in the league in passing, a statistic which will keep the Browns from winning any playoff games.

"When the opportunity for big plays presents itself," says Infante, "we're going to strike."

The only way the Browns offense was able to strike last year was on the ground. Kevin Mack (1,104 yards) and Earnest Byner (1,002) became the third running back tandem in National Football League history to each rush for over 1,000 yards. They almost single-handedly accounted for a come-from-behind victory against the Giants late in the season and their best years (both were 23) are still ahead.

To balance the offense, Schottenheimer drafted San Diego State speedster Webster Slaughter to provide a downfield target for Bernie Kosar's bombs. Kosar himself had a respectable, if not spectacular, rookie campaign. The University of Miami product completed 50 per cent of his passes and threw more touchdowns than interceptions. He even placed

Pittsburgh's Walter Abercrombie (previous pages main picture) follows a block as quarterback Mark Malone looks on. Rod Perry (far left) returns an interception as Bob Golic (left) watches from the sidelines. Bernie Kosar (below) turned in a solid rookie campaign with the help of backs Earnest Byner (facing page top) and Kevin Mack (facing page bottom right). Tom Cousineau (facing page bottom left) led a fine linebacking corps.

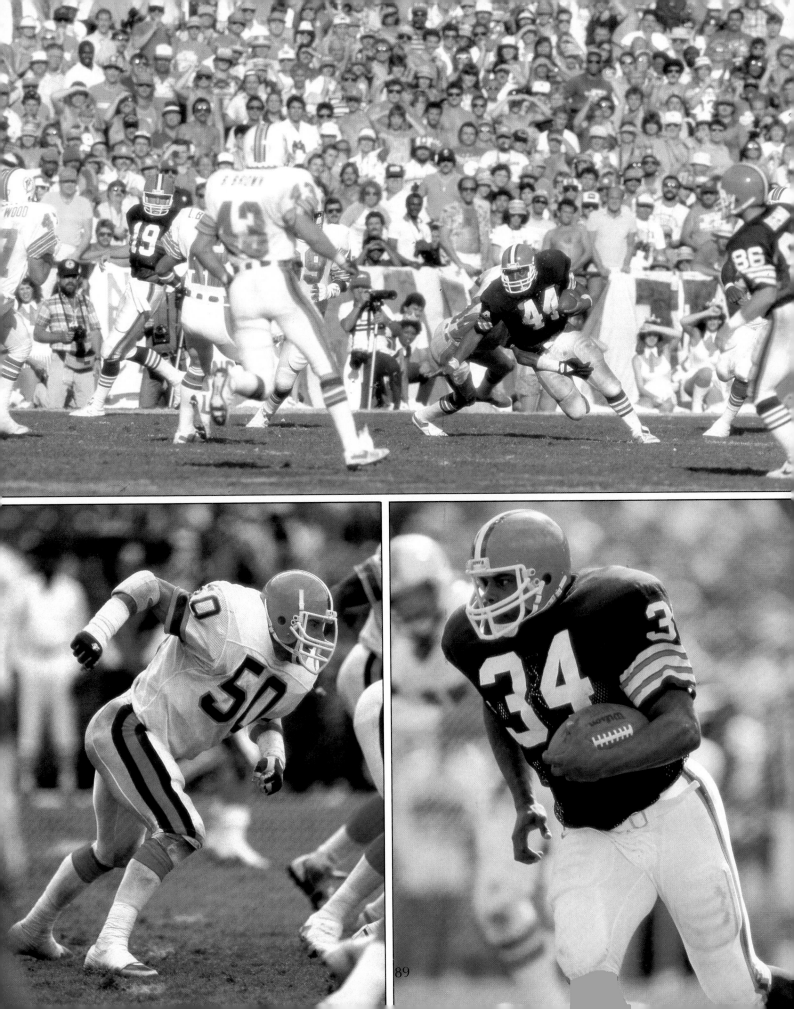

quarterback, a no-name defense and a losing record.

For the first time since 1971, the Steelers lost more games than they won and, for only the third time in the last 14 seasons, Pittsburgh failed to qualify for a post-season berth.

For veteran coach Chuck Noll, this will be the third time he's needed to reshape the team. When he took over in 1969, he made wholesale changes. In 1980 and 1981, Noll moved out the old veterans and brought in the kids. This season, his biggest task will be producing more offense.

Louis Lipps (facing page) turned into an all-pro receiver for the Steelers. Walter Abercrombie (left) turns the corner with a Charger in pursuit. Veteran defender Donnie Shell (above) takes a well-deserved breather. Mark Malone (overleaf insets top and bottom left) took over as Pittsburgh's quarterback as Sam Washington (inset bottom right) cheers him on. Abercrombie (main picture) tries to bull through the Miami defense.

just a point behind Denver quarterback John Elway in the QB ratings.

The only problem Kosar experienced, besides the tight reins placed on him by the coaching staff, was reading defenses. With a little more seasoning and winter-long skull sessions with Infante, Kosar should power the Browns to another Central Division crown.

Pittsburgh Steelers

When you envision the Pittsburgh Steelers, you see a team that wins the Central Division every year and has a spot locked up in the playoffs by Thanksgiving. Well, those were the old Pittsburgh Steelers, the ones with Franco and Mean Joe and Terry at the helm. The new Pittsburgh Steelers are the ones with Mark Malone at

The Steelers ranked 13th overall on offense and much of the improvement should come from Malone. Last season Malone began to take control of the offense until a toe injury forced him out of the lineup. Still, Malone threw almost twice as many touchdowns as interceptions (13-7) and handled the offense adequately.

Malone's biggest asset on offense

may be wide receiver Louis Lipps. Lipps, the former number one draft choice, made all-pro for the second straight season with leaping, acrobatic catches. He has scored 26 touchdowns in 30 NFL games, hauling in 59 passes a year ago. Lipps is joined by veteran wideout John Stallworth, who capped off one of his finest seasons with 75 receptions.

The defense was not the old Steel Curtain of the Super Bowl years, but it was a respectable unit which led the AFC after 13 games before slumping. The only problem the defense had was holding leads. Four times the Steelers were poised to win a game until the defense collapsed in the closing minutes.

Although Chuck Noll doesn't have the rebuilding job he did in 1969, don't expect the Steelers to be playing football past December.

Houston Oilers

With all the rhetoric and all the hype given to quarterback Warren Moon, one inescapable item re-emerges after each losing season in Houston. The defense, not Warren Moon, is more responsible for the lousy won-loss record.

Houston's million-dollar quarterback Warren Moon (above right and facing page) took a lot of the heat for the Oilers downfall in recent years, but a check of the statistics shows the problem isn't Moon as much as a poor defense. With Moon's cannon arm pitching bullets, the receivers (top and above left) better be prepared.

Since Bum Phillips left to coach the New Orleans Saints five years ago, the Houston defense has resided in the bottom eight of the league. Last season it finished a dismal 27th overall and dead last against the rush. Not only that, the defense sacked opposing quarterbacks but 42 times while intercepting just 15 passes, second worst total in the league.

Now back to Moon. He hasn't exactly had statisticians running for

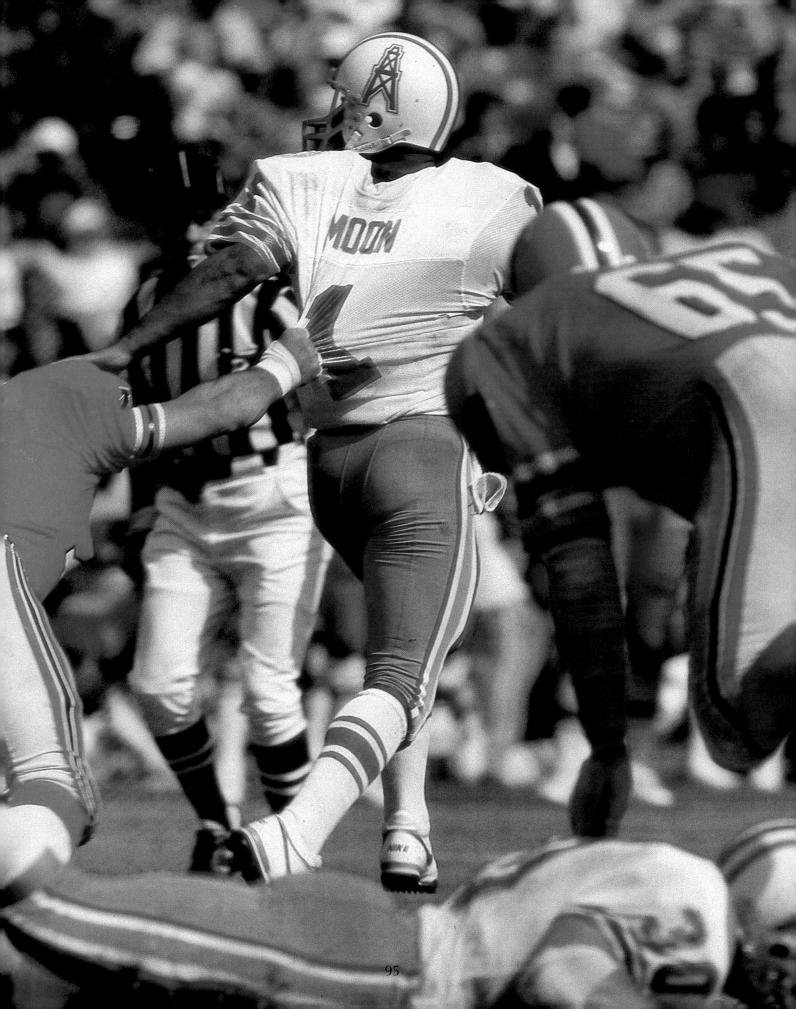

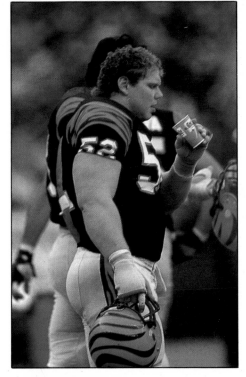

the record books since he arrived on the scene from Canada three years ago. Still, Moon spent much time on his back last year as the Oilers vaunted offensive line let opposing sackers get to Moon 58 times. "Needless to say, you can't play quarterback getting knocked down as much as our quarterbacks did last year," says Oilers coach Jerry Glanville. "More than anything, we have to stop talking about the ability and potential of our offensive line and look at how much they are producing."

Another area that needs to produce is the running game, where Houston finished 25th overall a year ago. Mike Rozier led the attack with a paltry 462 yards rushing while Butch Woolfolk caught 80 passes coming out of the backfield.

For Houston to make significant strides this season, many facets of their game must improve. And that may be asking too much, too soon.

Ken Anderson (facing page) is pressured by the Falcons' Al Richardson, but he was more pressured by young Boomer Esiason, who ultimately took his job. Ross Browner (above left) looks exasperated as the Bengals defense had trouble stopping anybody. Cris Collinsworth (above) hauls down a reception while offensive lineman Dave Rimington (left) takes a Gatorade break.

Cincinnati Bengals

The best way to sum up the Bengals defense in 1985 was, uh, offensive. It seemed every time the potent Cincinnati offense would put a touchdown on the board, the defense would trot off the field, shaking its heads after another opponent made a quick score.

The Bengals defense finished 22nd overall, but only 24th against the pass. The pass defense allowed a horrendous 64.7 pass completion percentage by the opposition while intercepting only 19 passes. The poor pass rush accounted for 40 sacks, an area the coaching staff expects to get better. "Pass rush and pressure on the passer may be the difference in the Bengals playoff hopes for 1986," says head coach Sam Wyche. "Our defensive line is dedicated to having a rebounding year this season."

The one area the Bengals don't have to rebound is on offense, where Boomer Esiason now runs the show. Esiason, a third year pro from Maryland, took the starting assignment from veteran Ken Anderson in the third game of the season and provided Cincinnati with an aerial display not seen this side of Air Coryell. Esiason finished the

Boomer Esiason (left) emerged as a star quarterback for the Bengals while John Stallworth (above) has always been a star for Pittsburgh. Warren Moon (facing page top and bottom left) led the Oilers offense at quarterback. Louis Lipps (facing page right) pushes off a Miami defender.

season with the second best quarterback rating (93.2), completing 251 of 431 passes for 27 touchdowns and only 12 interceptions.

The improved running game had much to do with Esiason's success in the air as it finished 12th in the league

overall. James Brooks came to the fore, gaining 929 yards with seven touchdowns, while massive Larry Kinnebrew ran his bulky body through the line for 714 yards and nine TDs.

When you talk about mass, though, you talk about the offensive line. Anthony Munoz (6-6, 278) anchors one of the best lines in football that includes Mike Wilson (6-5, 271), Max Montoya (6-5, 275), Brian Blados (6-4, 295) and Dave Rimington (6-3, 280).

If the defense can come close to matching the offense's production, the Bengals will be a playoff team.

AFC WEST DIVISION

Denver Broncos

The Denver Broncos may have been the NFL team that accomplished the most yet accomplished the least in 1985. Don't understand, huh? Well for one, the Broncos made great strides in consistency on offense as John Elway's maturing process continued. They overcame obstacles to finish the season with a fine record of 11-5. Yet, even with that mark, they couldn't nudge themselves into the playoffs despite having a much better record than the 8-8 Central Division champion Browns.

"This is a big year for us," admits Denver coach Dan Reeves, who has guided the Broncs to 24 wins in two seasons. "If we can have some of our younger players step forward, and we don't drop off in our performance level, then we're going to be a good, solid team this year."

One of the younger players Reeves expects to step forward is Elway, the former number one pick in 1983. The first two seasons with the Broncos, Elway struggled for consistency. Sure he had the cannon arm and sure he could hit the long bomb, but just as sure he could throw an interception. As last season progressed, Elway showed signs that this might be the year the Stanford graduate moves to the top of the quarterback class.

"John Elway made tremendous strides again last year," Reeves says. "We didn't have a balanced running game to take the pressure off John last year, and he had a lot of pressure on him all season."

Elway finished the campaign with 3,891 yards passing, second only to Dan Marino and first in total offense with 4,144 yards.

With Elway maturing on offense, it was up to the defense to provide a steady hand. And they did. Led by linebacker Karl Mecklenburg, the Broncos were in every game. In fact, 11 of the 16 games they played were decided in the last few minutes. Mecklenburg didn't start for Denver until the 10th game, yet the third-year player was named a starter for the Pro Bowl. Mecklenburg registered a team record 13 sacks, forced five fumbles and even played seven positions on defense.

This season, with Mecklenburg starting from the outset and Elway primed for prime time, the Broncos won't be watching the playoffs on television.

Los Angeles Raiders

No matter what happens to the Raiders, there's one constant that you can count on – a winning team. The 1985 version proved that, even in a rebuilding season, the Raiders are a team to be reckoned with, as evidenced by their glitzy 12-4 record and 13th Western Division crown.

Previous pages: the NFL's all-time leading receiver, Charlie Joiner (inset) also has a bubbly personality. Dave Krieg (main picture) fires to a receiver. Denver's QB John Elway (left) tucks it in. Billy Johnson (facing page top) complains to an official. The Denver defense (facing page bottom) created many loose balls.

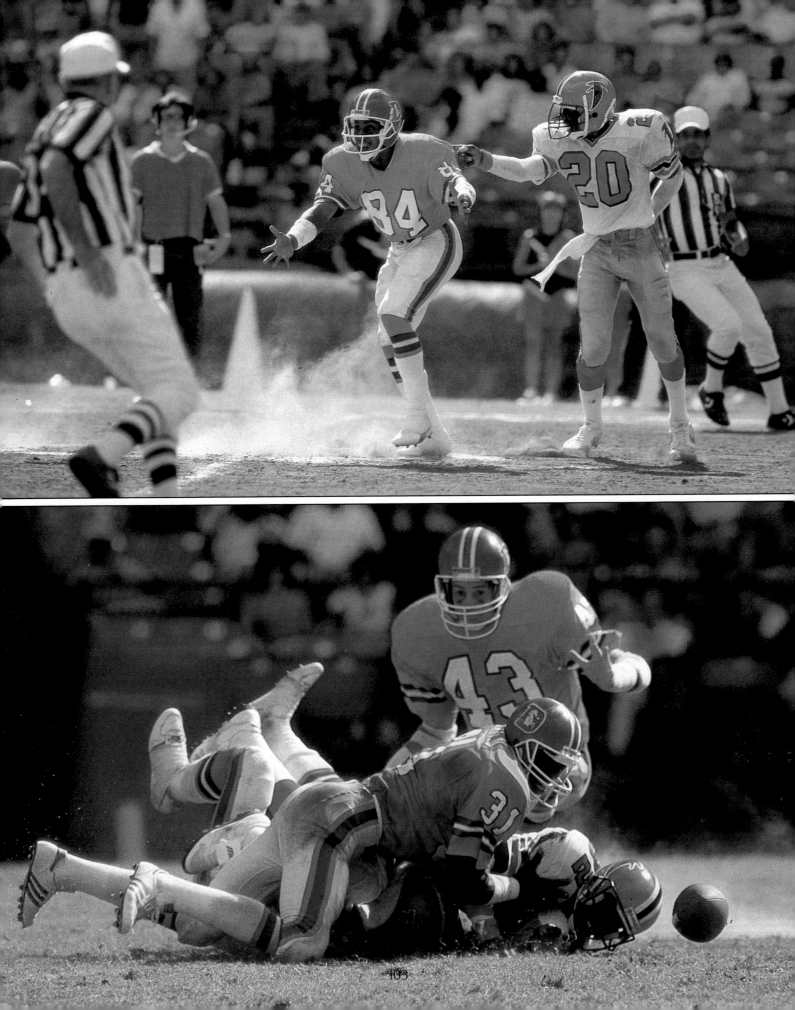

Seven new starters were eased into the lineup last season but, as usual, there was no drop in quality. Dokie Williams and rookie Jessie Hester took over the wide receiver positions with outstanding results. Williams caught 48 passes for 925 yards while Hester's 20.8 yards per catch average was the best among

Previous pages: kicker Rich Karlis and his holder (main picture) study the trajectory of the ball on a field goal attempt. A measurement is needed (insets left – and bottom right!) while an official signals a touchdown (inset top right). Howie Long (facing page) shows the form that made him an all-pro. Lester Hayes' ability as a defensive back (below and below right) make the Raiders cheerleader (right) ecstatic.

rookie wideouts. Don Mosebar, a first round pick from the University of Southern California in 1983, moved in as a starter at center without many problems.

Defensively, four new starters continued the Raiders tradition of excellence and aggression. Bill Pickel took over at middle guard and went on to lead the team in sacks with 12½ and the defensive line in tackles with 93. Reggie McKenzie stepped into the inside linebacker slot, started every game and even recorded 17 tackles in the playoff loss to New England. With Lyle Alzado injured (now retired), Sean Jones performed admirably at defensive right end, recording 8½ sacks in the regular season and a pair in the playoffs. The final newcomer

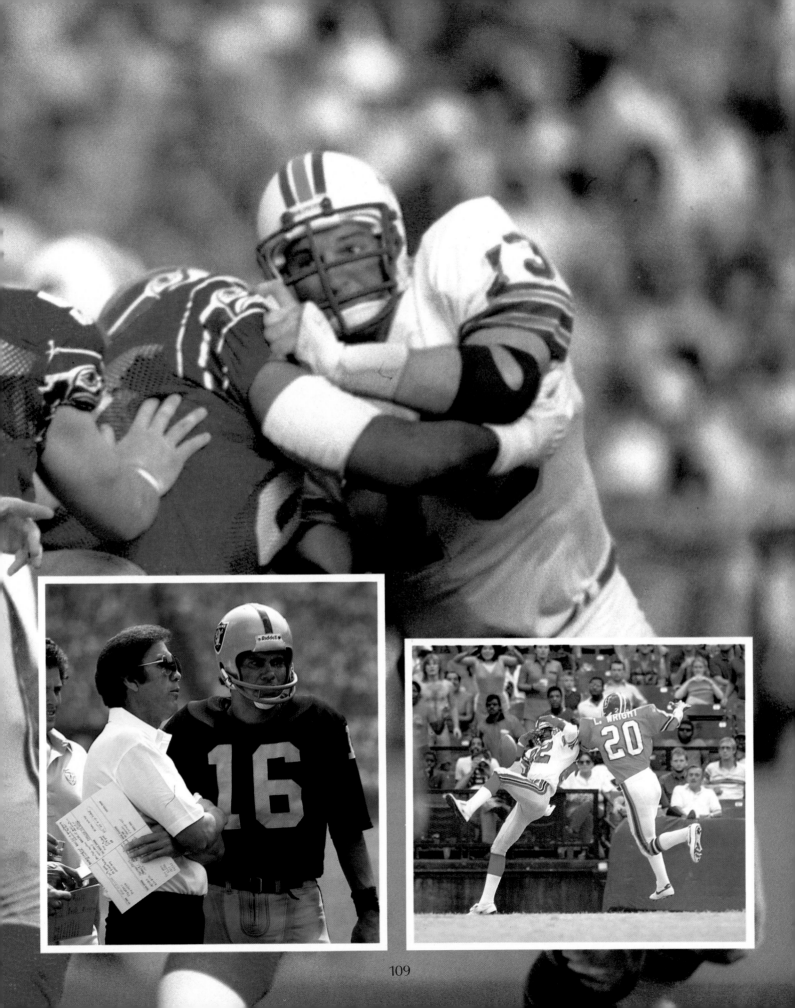

was Stacey Toran, who played 11 games at safety and even returned an interception 76 yards for a touchdown against the New York Jets.

All was not new with the Raiders as Marcus Allen had his greatest season as a pro, setting an NFL record for most combined yards from scrimmage (2,314) on 1,759 yards rushing and 555 receiving. His rushing total also led the NFL.

With the new foundation set in place, the winning tradition will continue for the Los Angeles Raiders.

Seattle Seahawks

All was not well for the Seattle Seahawks in 1985. Predicted to be a division winner by some, a Super Bowl participant by others, the Seahawks went backwards last year, finishing a dismal 8-8.

There could be many fingers pointed for the reason the Hawks slipped from contender to pretender, but the primary one pointed directly to the offense. Quarterback Dave Krieg suffered through an inconsistent season, although his numbers were impressive. Krieg tied for second in the NFL in touchdown passes with 27 and completed nearly 54 per cent of his passes. Yet, when Krieg made a mistake, it was costly and, with 20 interceptions, Krieg made many mistakes.

Another reason the Seahawks offense finished as only the 18th best in the league was Curt Warner. Don't think this as a knock on Warner, who rebounded from serious knee surgery in '84 to have a fine '85 campaign. Because Warner possesses marvelous talents, defenses geared their game plan toward stopping Warner and, when they did, Seattle had nobody else to turn to in the backfield. While the former Penn State flash rushed for over 1,000 yards for the second time, fullback David Hughes ran for only 128 yards, seven more than Krieg.

To try and ease the burden on Warner, Seattle used its first pick in the draft for fullback John L. Williams, a legitimate threat out of the backfield with 4.6 speed.

"All of a sudden our short-yardage game rises, our play action becomes more effective and lanes open up a lot

Previous pages: Dave Krieg (main picture) spots a receiver (inset center left) who hauls it in. John Elway (inset left) had a safe season for the Broncos while his counterpart in Los Angeles, Jim Plunkett (inset center right) missed most of the season with an injury. Louis Wright (inset right) clobbers a Falcon receiver. Krieg (top) to Steve Largent (above) has been a potent combination for Seattle. The Seahawk defense (facing page) wasn't as intimidating as in the past.

wider for Curt," acknowledges Seahawks backfield coach Chick Harris.

The defense was not as sour as the offense, although it did take a turn for the worse last season. Still, the Hawks ranked 11th overall, ninth against the rush and tied for sixth in interceptions.

With an improved offense bolstered by a dynamic backfield and a steady defense, look for Seattle to turn some heads in 1986. This time, though, it will be for the better.

Kansas City Chiefs

Hopefully for Todd Blackledge, 1986 will prove to the Kansas City Chiefs that they didn't get gyped when they chose Blackledge ahead of Dan Marino, Tony Eason, Jim Kelly and Ken O'Brien in the great quarterback draft of 1983. Those four QBs, along with the number one pick in that draft, John Elway, have taken their teams to the top, whether its the NFL or USFL (in Kelly's case). Now it's Blackledge's turn to try.

To all intents and purposes, the Chiefs have handed the quarterback job to Blackledge. "The biggest thing about the quarterback position in 1985 is the fact that Todd Blackledge showed he was able to play in the starting role, accomplish some things and play well," said Chiefs coach John Mackovic.

Indeed he did. While not punching up sterling statistics, Blackledge did hit on 50 per cent of his passes and throw for more than 1,000 yards in limited duty. His only problem was interceptions, tossing 14, more than twice as many as TD passes (6).

If Blackledge is to succeed, he'll need a running game that was virtually non-existent last season. Herman Heard, who rambled for 595 yards, led the squad that finished last in the NFL a year ago. The Chiefs tried to bolster that weakness with its first round draft pick, hulking offensive lineman Brian Jozwiak, a 6-5½ 309-pounder from West Virginia. Besides his physical prowess, Jozwiak has the attitude the Chiefs love. "I try to play every down like it's the last," Jozwiak said. "I'm willing to go out and spill everything I have."

The Kansas City defense should

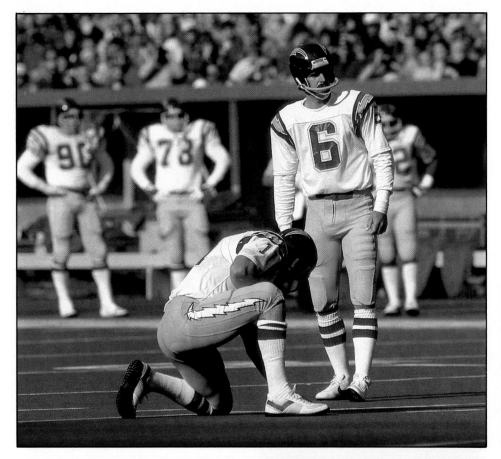

receivers as easily as he puts on his socks and bang! The Chargers would score. The only differences in the defense now are the names.

And surprise, surprise. The San Diego Chargers finished first in overall offense and dead last in defense. That translated into an 8-8 campaign for the boys from the west.

The only change for Fouts was the arsenal he used to dissect the opposition. With Kellen Winslow on the mend for much of the season, Fouts used pint-sized half back Lionel James coming out of the backfield. James merely led the conference with 86 receptions. Another newcomer,

also adopt that attitude because after last season's 20th place ranking, it needs all the help it could get. That help could come from Walt Corey, although it won't be on the field. Corey is the new defensive coordinator and, with the talent he has to work with, the Chiefs defense should start scalping people again.

But in a tough division like this, it won't be enough.

San Diego Chargers

Close your eyes and think back to 1975. There was Dan Fouts shredding enemy defenses the way Chernobyl lit up the Soviet Union. First down or fourth down, it didn't matter. The Chargers would go back to pass, Fouts would spot a receiver and bang! Touchdown. Now think about the defense. With Fouts on the sidelines, the defense would come in and keep the opposition offense amused until a tying touchdown was scored.

Now open your eyes. It's 10 years later, 1985, and nothing has changed. Fouts still eases back into the pocket close to 40 times a game, spots his

Seattle's David Hughes (previous pages) finds the going tough against the Dolphins. San Diego's Rolf Benirschke lines up a field goal try (top). Mike Green (above) fights off Ted Peterson as Joiner (above right) looks on.

Gary Anderson contributed mightily, catching 35 passes and rushing for over 400 yards. When the season ended for Fouts, he wound up ranked first among active players in passing yards and third all-time behind a couple of pretty good quarterbacks, Fran Tarkenton and Johnny Unitas.

The only records the defense hold are for futility. As coach Don Coryell says, "We need defense. We have to take the ball away from people. Defenses have changed so much that it takes longer to develop a defense. I think you will be shocked at how much our defensive players improve. I have confidence that the defensive players are going to get much better."

They had better. Or another .500 campaign looms ahead.

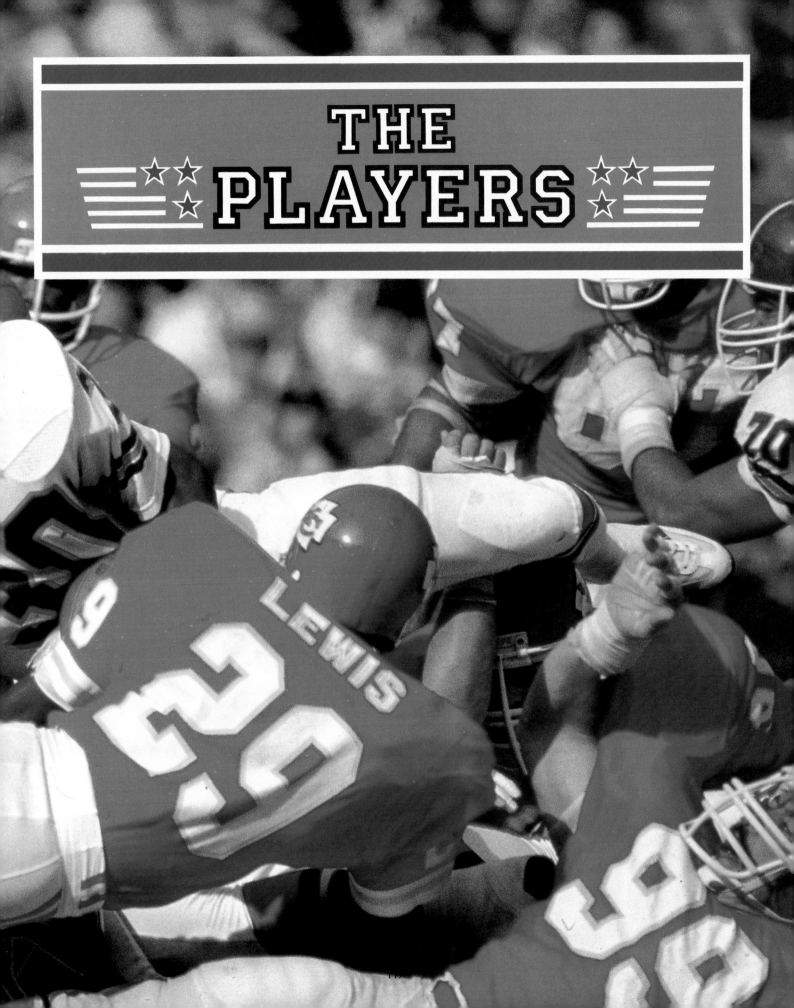

THE PLAYERS

THE QUARTER-BACKS

Dan Marino

The similarities are apparent and therefore the comparisons are inevitable. Every time Dan Marino fades back to pass you can see it. The deep drop, the radar-like eyes moving back and forth, searching out the defense and looking for that open receiver. At the last moment, with defenders the size of redwoods bearing down, all it takes is a flick of the wrist. And like a pea shot out of a cannon, the football is heading for its destination. The defenders are draped all over the receivers, but that doesn't matter. The ball still finds its target.

Every time Dan Marino fades back to pass, you can even feel it. The confidence that no matter what happens, the job will get done. The swagger that says "I am the best." Although they are very different off the field, Dan Marino, a future Hall-of-Famer, is very similar to a present Hall-of-Famer Joe Namath.

"Dan's got an outgoing, attack-type personality," says his coach Don Shula. "He's a winner because he's not afraid to do the things you have to do to win. He's like Joe Namath in that respect."

"I've been up in the press box watching him play and he throws a ball he had absolutely no business throwing right into double or triple coverage," says former Miami Dolphin quarterback Bob Griese. "But it ends up being a touchdown. He leaves you no margin for error but he almost always gets away with it. He has so much confidence in his arm and his receivers. It's almost a false sense of security. You know, I think Joe Namath was like that."

Joe Namath may have been like that, but he never put the numbers on the board the way Dan Marino has for the Miami Dolphins in his first three years in the NFL. Namath may have been the first quarterback to ever pass for over 4,000 yards in a season, but Marino is the first to ever pass for more than 5,000 yards in a season. He established NFL records for completion percentage by a rookie (58.45), most passes completed in a season (362), most 300-yard games in a season (9) and most 400-yard games in a season (4). Marino's most

shocking record may be the 48 touchdown passes he threw in the 1984 campaign, shattering George Blanda and Y.A. Tittle's mark of 36 touchdown passes.

"Hey, I think I can complete any pass I throw and we can score any time we go out on the field," says the 6-4, 215-pound Marino. "Otherwise why go out there?"

He did exactly that in his junior season with the Pittsburgh Panthers, when he was the most highly regarded quarterback in the country. Scouts soured on him in his senior year when an arm injury and unsubstantiated rumors of drug use ruined his season. Those were the reasons Marino didn't get drafted until the 27th pick in the first round although, incredibily, five quarterbacks were selected before him.

"On draft day," Marino recalls, "I was sitting there not believing that so many players were going ahead of me. But my dad always said things happen for a reason. Maybe it's fate that I went so late and that it worked out so well."

That may be the understatement of a lifetime. Marino stepped into a

Joe Montana (previous page main picture) and John Elway (inset) passed their teams to the top. Dan Marino (above) takes instructions from Don Shula. Facing page: Ken O'Brien.

situation where the Dolphins were a contending team, just coming off a Super Bowl loss to the Washington Redskins. He could be worked into the lineup easily and, with Don Shula calling the shots, Marino received the guidance he needed to become a star.

Marino played in only 11 games in his rookie season, but he still threw for 2,210 yards, 20 touchdowns and only seven interceptions. It was only a prelude of what was to come. In his second season, Marino was such a terror that even the sophomore jinx was scared of him. He ripped apart opposing defenses weekly, leading the league in attempts (564), completions (362), yards (5,084), touchdown passes (48) and average per completion (9.01) while taking the Dolphins to the Super Bowl against the San Francisco 49ers.

"He's such a competitor," says Denver Broncos scout George Karras. "He goes for the jugular. He throws an interception, there's no throwing of a helmet, no look of disgust. He'll go back and throw into the same coverage and throw a touchdown and that's what separates him from the pack."

"Some day," says Dolphins' wide receiver Mark Duper, the target for many Marino bombs, "Marino is going to throw for 700 yards and no one on this team will be surprised."

Least of all Marino.

Ken O'Brien

It was not an easy beginning to a professional career for Ken O'Brien. Consider the circumstances: the New York Jets, with the 24th selection in the first round, admittedly desire a young quarterback for the future, to learn behind veteran Richard Todd. With four quarterbacks already taken, the pick would be an easy one for the Jets. Sitting on the board, still available, was Dan Marino, the rifle-armed signalcaller for the Panthers of Pitt. The match was perfect. Marino was an east coast kid, born in Pittsburgh, the kind of high-profile quarterback New Yorkers would take to.

The fans at the Sheraton Hotel in New York were howling Marino's name, but that chanting was nothing compared to the screaming outrage heard a few minutes later when commissioner Pete Rozelle announced the Jets selection as Ken O'Brien, an obscure quarterback from Division II Cal-Davis.

"You guys got brain damage or something," bellowed an unhappy Jets' fan to the New York table. "This is the first round, not the 12th."

Personnel Director Mike Hickey, though, emerged all smiles after the pick. "He's a great prospect," he said at the time. "He's better than Marino, in my opinion. He has a better arm, better field vision. He's intelligent, poised, competitive. He has everything you look for."

"If you saw the films, you wouldn't be asking about him being a Division II quarterback," coach Joe Walton said. "We feel he's our quarterback of the future."

Walton certainly knew something when he said "the future" because O'Brien did not play a single down in

his rookie season. In fact, even in his second season, O'Brien played in only 10 games, completing 57.1 per cent of his passes. But in his third season, the Jets let loose on the reins and O'Brien blossomed into one of the finest quarterbacks in the league, leading the Jets to an 11-5 record and a berth in the playoffs.

"Last year, he was feeling his way along," says Jets backup QB Pat Ryan, who lost his job to O'Brien. "Now, he's doing things just by feel. That's the way it happens. It's like groping in the dark for the switch, and then you learn where it is and the light goes on, so to speak."

There was no question that O'Brien lit up opposing defenses as he finished the season as the top rated quarterback in the NFL with a 96.2 rating. The 6-4, 210-pound O'Brien completed 60.9 per cent of his passes for 3,888 yards and 25 touchdowns. Perhaps his most important accomplishment is throwing only eight interceptions, with the lowest interception percentage (1.6) in the league.

"I think Kenny's doing just about what we thought he'd do when we scouted him," Hickey says. "It simply takes a little time."

And a little work. Following his sophomore campaign, O'Brien realized he needed to improve his quickness and ability to avoid a pass rush. In the off-season, he trimmed down and the results were almost immediate.

"He's matured a lot," says Jets tight end Mickey Shuler. "He's settled down and he's working at it. He realizes now what he wants. He has himself organized. His goals are set. Before he was unsure what he wanted to do."

"It takes a lot of hard work and long hours," O'Brien concedes. "You've got to be dedicated to it. A lot of times I'd much rather be doing something else. But you have to work."

The work was done with Jets quarterback coach Zeke Bratkowski, who tutored him and gave the light-haired signalcaller the confidence he needed.

"You have to be assertive," says Bratkowski. "You have to be totally in control of the system. You can't be a cheerleader until after the completion."

"No doubt, Zeke is one of the best things that ever happened to me," O'Brien admits. "Zeke hasn't changed anything drastic. He's made me concentrate on details. I understand what everyone's going to do on a play. If I make a tackler miss, I don't have to say, 'OK, who's open?' I know where to look.

"I feel confident that whatever I say, it's going to work. I don't think I changed my style. What I'm trying to do is solve all the ifs.

"You have to have fun on the weekend and we're going to go out and have fun."

The only people who won't be having fun are the defenders trying to stop him.

Joe Montana

The scene is one of hundreds in the career of Joe Montana, but it is one that is repeated more often than "The Wizard of Oz." Joe Montana stands behind the San Francisco center and barks out the play. He takes the snaps and backpedals as smoothly as Willie Mays did tracking down a long fly to centerfield. Montana comes to a halt, looks left then right. The 6-2, 195-pound Notre Dame alumnus begins to feel a pass rush and slowly starts rolling out of the pocket. With a behemoth defensive end charging him from behind, Montana turns it up a notch, keeping a safe distance.

Now the entire defense is in hot pursuit. Montana pump fakes to a receiver, enabling himself another split second. Fading towards the sideline, Montana can almost feel the hot breath of a linebacker in front of him and a big, taped paw of a defensive end reaching for him from the side. With a flick of the wrist, he sends a spiral downfield. A moment later, the defenders meet with Montana in the middle of an unsavory collision. The ball, however, is safely tucked into the hands of a receiver and the 49ers continue their march toward the end zone.

For seven years, that has been the modus operandi of Joe Montana. The quick feet. The elusiveness. The extra split second. It's Joe Montana's game

and it's been a successful one. Since coming to the Niners in 1979, Montana has led the Niners to two Super Bowl victories including two Most Valuable Player awards, a conference championship and a host of division titles.

"It's a relief to run down the field and see nothing but trouble, everything getting very hairy and as you turn your head you see Joe Montana scrambling," says San Francisco tight end Russ Francis. "He has seen the problem before you get there and now he's going to finish the play anyway. And you know he will finish it."

"Joe Montana knows how important his feet are," says 49ers quarterback coach Paul Hackett. "Over a period of six weeks going over game films, we might have mentioned his feet three times. Last year on only five passes did his feet cost him an interception. That's just unbelieveable."

Almost as unbelievable as the plethora of records Montana has registered in his career. He holds the career mark for highest passer rating (92.7), highest completion percentage (63) and lowest interception percentage (2.6). And to think, Montana wasn't drafted until the third round because of his inconsistent play and a shoulder injury which left scouts dubious of his arm.

"I knew of his inconsistency," San Francisco coach Bill Walsh says. "I also knew about his competitiveness. If he could be great for one game, why not two, why not repetition? He was willing to learn. That was easy to tell. I knew he would improve. I was anxious to zero in on this guy."

Along with his competitiveness, Montana is a field general, a take-charge guy, an asset that's almost necessary to be a winning quarterback.

"I try to react positively by projecting an upbeat feeling in the huddle," says Montana. "I want to project a feeling of confidence to the receiver who I think I'm going to end up throwing to."

Montana (facing page) is the NFL's all-time leader in quarterback ratings (92.7), completion percentage (63.0) and interception percentage (2.6).

"I'm not a fiery guy, but when I'm on the field I have to know exactly what has to be done and how to get everybody to do it. I guess it has become second nature to me because I have been doing it since high school. You have to know you are right and if you are wrong, you have to act like you're right, at least until the coach yells at you."

"There's not a lot of lemmings on this team," says Niners guard Randy Cross. "So Joe Montana's your perfect field general for a bunch of individualistic maniacs. No rah, rah. His leadership has come slowly, by example. He's always thinking a step ahead."

"Joe has been an extremely consistent performer who has come up with big efforts in the big games," Walsh says. "He leads the team by example, and is the ultimate in modern-day quarterbacks. He stretches our limits. He redefines what is sensible."

Montana continued that redefining a year ago as he topped the National Football Conference in passing with a 91.3 rating, third in the NFL. He finished second behind Dan Marino in touchdown passes with 27 and threw only 13 interceptions. At age 30, Joe Montana is just reaching his peak. And that's bad news for the rest of the league.

Jim McMahon

"Heck, if I was 6-4 and 280, I'd be a lineman. I could have a good time doing that." – Jim McMahon

To say that Jim McMahon is not your stereotypical quarterback is tantamount to saying that Eddie Murphy is just another funny guy. It goes deeper than that. Much deeper. Jim McMahon is strange even for a football player. He has a spiked haircut, wears sunglasses all the time and carries an attitude that ranks with the cockiest players in the game.

He's the guy who reported to his team on draft day with a can of beer in his hand. He's the guy who bucked authority by wearing a handband with "Rozelle" written on it, just to annoy the commissioner. He's the guy who wore a priest's shirt that had a collar and no back when Bears coach Mike

Montana (previous page all pictures) is a cool general for the 49ers. "I'm not a fiery guy," he says, "but when I'm on the field I have to know exactly what has to be done and how to get everybody to do it." Jim McMahon (facing page and above) sometimes tests the patience of coach Mike Ditka (right).

Ditka required shirts with collars on team flights. He's the guy who gave a national television audience the finger salute. He's the guy who, oh well, you get the idea.

"He likes to be disgusting on purpose, just to get a reaction out of people," says Chicago wide receiver Ken Margerum. "It gives him a kind of mystique. I think that's healthy."

"There are a lot of people outside the locker room who wonder about Jim – whether he's too cocky or this or

that," says Bears veteran safety Gary Fencik. "I think that all that really matters is that Jim is a helluva quarterback who consistently performs on Sunday and isn't into developing a more positive public image. I don't really see that he views P.R. as being part of the job."

The only part that McMahon feels is important is playing quarterback, and McMahon even has different thoughts about that.

"I don't like all the rules about you can't hit quarterbacks," McMahon says. "Jack Lambert (former Pittsburgh Steelers linebacker) had the right idea when he said to put dresses on them all. Most of the quarterbacks don't like to get hit. Better not play this game if you don't want to get hit. I don't mind getting hit. I like pain at times."

Pain is something only his opponents felt last year as McMahon guided the Bears to their first championship in 22 years. The 27-year-old quarterback expertly engineered the Chicago offense, finishing second in the NFC in passing, completing 56.9 per cent of his throws. Aside from statistics, McMahon gave the Bears something intangible – the desire to win at all costs.

That was apparent during a Monday night game when McMahon rode the bench because of muscle spasms and a leg infection. With Chicago trailing 17-9 in the third period, McMahon entered the game. His first two passes were for touchdowns and his third TD pass came five plays later. After 5½ minutes with McMahon in the contest, the Bears were ahead 30-17.

The one aspect of his game that simply makes coach Mike Ditka cringe is his total disregard for his body. Instead of running out of bounds, McMahon will greet his tacklers head-on. Instead of resting with an injury, McMahon will push to the limit. He's shown his teammates that being crazy is the way to be.

"I think the biggest thing I did for this team was to bring their personalities out of the closet," McMahon says. "We've got a lot of guys that were here when I first came and they were kind of holding back it seemed. They saw what a fool I was, I shaved my head, I didn't care. You just can't worry about what other people think. I don't. You don't have to be a robot, and we had a lot of robots."

McMahon came to the Bears in 1982 as the fifth player selected in the first round of the draft. The 6-0, 187-pounder was a product of Brigham Young University, of all schools. A strict Mormon college, McMahon found himself in trouble all the time at BYU. His major difficulty concerned the Code of Honor, which every student attending the university must sign and which lists alcohol consumption among its prohibitions. The only difficulty he didn't have was passing the football as McMahon set 71 major college records.

Even with those credentials, McMahon encountered problems with the Bears, who were upset with his practice habits.

"I had confidence in my abilities and given a chance, I knew I could compete," he remembers. "But you see, I'm not the best practice player. When I first reported to the Bears I was in terrible shape. I couldn't even run a mile and a half. When I didn't practice great, I didn't open very many eyes, but once I performed in the games, they thought maybe this guy's for real."

Nobody has to think about that any more. McMahon has answered those questions in his own special way.

John Elway

It was supposed to be so easy. There was John Elway, the owner of a plethora of college football passing records, the man with the rifle arm, quick feet and Yale mentality. A natural. Not many rookie quarterbacks have ever stepped into the starting lineup and taken their team to the top. But this was to be different. This was John Elway. The greatest prospect to enter pro football in years. He was, to Denver fans, the savior.

"For five months, every day, there was a front-page story on him," says former Denver Broncos quarterback coach John Hadl. "I had never seen anything like it. Things like, 'Elway threw 97 passes in practice today... 2 dropped, 2 overthrown.' It was ridiculous. Every other headline had 'Super Bowl' in it.'"

Denver coach Dan Reeves didn't make things any easier on the kid from Stanford. Most young quarterbacks are allowed a grace period, a time to stand on the sidelines and learn, digest a new offensive system and watch a more experienced signalcaller. Ken O'Brien did it. In his first season with the Jets, O'Brien didn't see action for even one play. But Elway, the five million dollar man, was thrown to the lions.

It wasn't until the Bears, however, that Reeves finally realized his mistake. On October 2, 1983, Elway started against Chicago. He threw 10 passes that day, completed 4 for a measly 36 yards. Finally Reeves pulled him from the game and Denver went on to an embarrassing 31-14 defeat. It was the lowest point of Elway's young career.

"I got caught up in things," remembers Elway. "There was so much hype early that I was the savior of the Denver Broncos. It bothered me. Then the frustrations of failing worked against me. The worse things went, the more bad things that were said and the harder I tried. I put too much pressure on myself.

"As much as I said it didn't bother me, things got to me. It's a terrible feeling to drop back and not know what's going on in front of you, but that's how it goes for a rookie quarterback in this league. The Chicago game was the bottom.

"I worried about remembering the plays. I worried about calling the formations and getting the play off without a delay-of-the-game penalty. I couldn't even think about the defense."

"My mistake," acknowledges Reeves. "They started throwing defenses at John that I hadn't seen before. His knowledge of the offense was memory, not understanding. When he came into a game situation, the language wasn't normal. He couldn't just say, 'Red Right, Power 48-G-O.' He had to think. It was all he could do to get the snap off, and everything after the snap was a complete surprise. It was like learning a language. He had an idea what was being said, but he couldn't speak it himself. There's no question if I had it to do over again, that I would not have started him."

Luckily, this story has a happy ending. Sure Elway struggled badly in his first campaign. He played in 11 games, completing 123 passes in 259 attempts for a poor 47.535 percentage. His ratio of touchdown passes to interceptions, 7 to 14, was something out of a Stephen King nightmare. But the talent was there, even if it only flashed sporadically.

His second campaign brought a new John Elway. He spent the off-

John Elway (facing page) matured greatly in 1985, setting Bronco season records for attempts (605), completions (327), passing yards (3,891), total rushing and passing plays (656) and total offense (4,144 yards).

season with the playbook under his arm, with his eyes fixed on a film projector. For the first time in his life, Elway studied for his football final exams. In college, he was so advanced that his natural talent took over. In 1984, Elway took his first few strides toward his destiny.

"John has done more work from the end of football season than anyone in the league," says Broncos offensive coordinator Mike Shanahan. "He is very serious about wanting to be the best."

"The difference between John in his second year and John in his rookie year was obvious in the huddle," says veteran wide receiver Steve Watson. "John takes the game to the limit. He showed he was destined for stardom."

"He came through in crucial situations and we gained an awful lot of confidence in John," Reeves says. "If you're looking for lots of acrobatic touchdowns like (Dan) Marino, well, he didn't do that. But we didn't have (Mark) Clayton and (Mark) Duper for wide-outs."

Facing page: Elway raises up from the line of scrimmage to call a timeout. "He came through in crucial situations and we gained an awful lot of confidence in John," says coach Dan Reeves (above). "If you're looking for lots of acrobatic touchdidn't do that. But we didn't have (Mark) Clayton and (Mark) Duper for wide-outs."

Elway's second season was nothing to complain about. He played 15 games, hit 56.3 per cent of his passes and threw for over 2,500 yards. The biggest improvement, however, was in his touchdown-interception ratio. Elway tossed 18 TD passes and threw but 15 interceptions. He also showed his athletic ability by rushing for 237 yards on 56 carries. The elements for stardom were there – and fast approaching.

"I hate to fail" Elway says. "My rookie year was the first time I'd ever been faced with something where nothing came easy. In college I could make up for my lack of understanding through my ability to play. In the NFL you can't do that.

"My second year the confidence started coming back. I was getting to the point where I could just go out and react, I could just compete and be myself. I knew what was going on. I know the greatness will come, I just need to keep that as my goal."

Before his third season in the league his star was rising and other coaches were noticing. A comment by Cincinnati coach Sam Wyche turned out to be quite prophetic.

"Elway is bordering on a Marino-type year. Nobody plays Denver without worrying if that could be the game Elway explodes. John is a time bomb waiting to go off."

And that time bomb went off many times last season and sometimes it was more like a nuclear explosion. Elway burst onto the scene big-time, leading Denver to several last-minute victories. The poise, something missing his first two campaigns, was there. The soft touch, a commodity Elway didn't bring into the NFL, emerged. Nineteen eighty-five was the year the NFL saw the real John Elway.

The former number one pick set Bronco single season records for attempts (605, which led the NFL), completions (327, second in the NFL), passing yards (3,891, second to Marino in the league), total rushing and passing plays (656, which led the NFL) and total offense (4,144, which also led the league). In addition, Elway rushed for 253 yards, which led all AFC quarterbacks.

He finished the '85 season with a string of seven consecutive games in which he threw a touchdown pass and, by directing Denver to a fine 11-5 record, he upped his overall winning percentage to second only to Dan Marino's 25-6 mark for the Dolphins.

"John Elway made tremendous strides again last year," Reeves says. "He had a season in which he played with some hurts but did not miss any playing time.

"We didn't have a balanced running game to take the pressure off John last year and he had a lot of pressure on him all season long. John just did a great job leading us to 11 wins. I look forward to him improving even more next year."

Now that's the way its supposed to be.

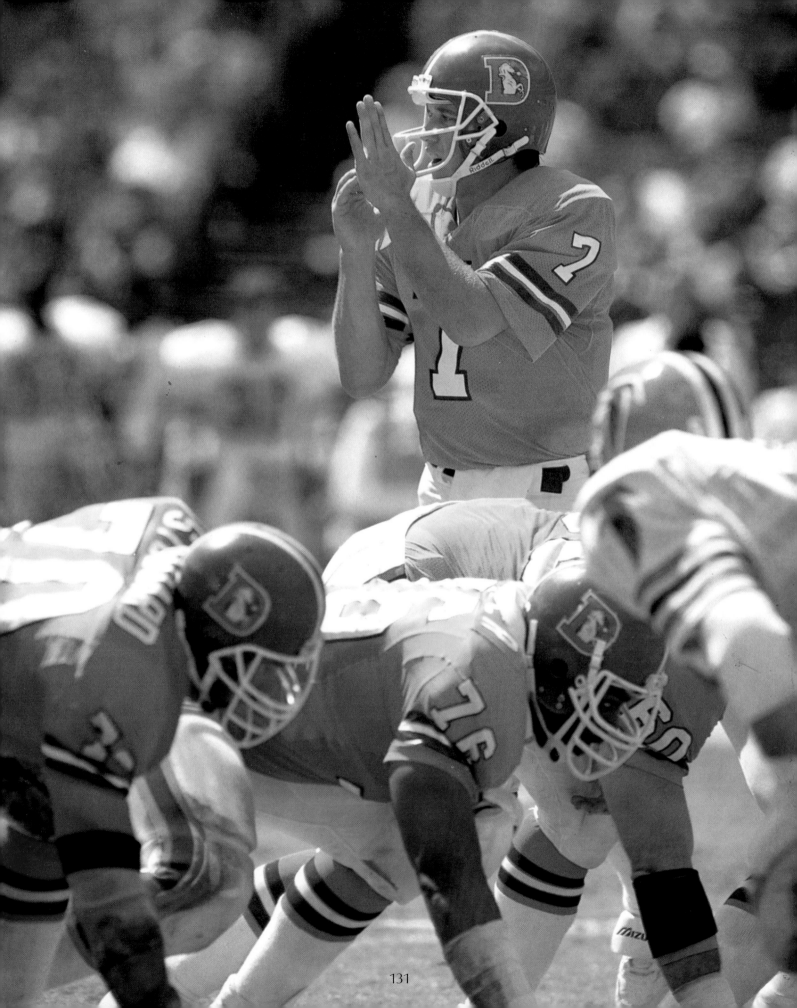

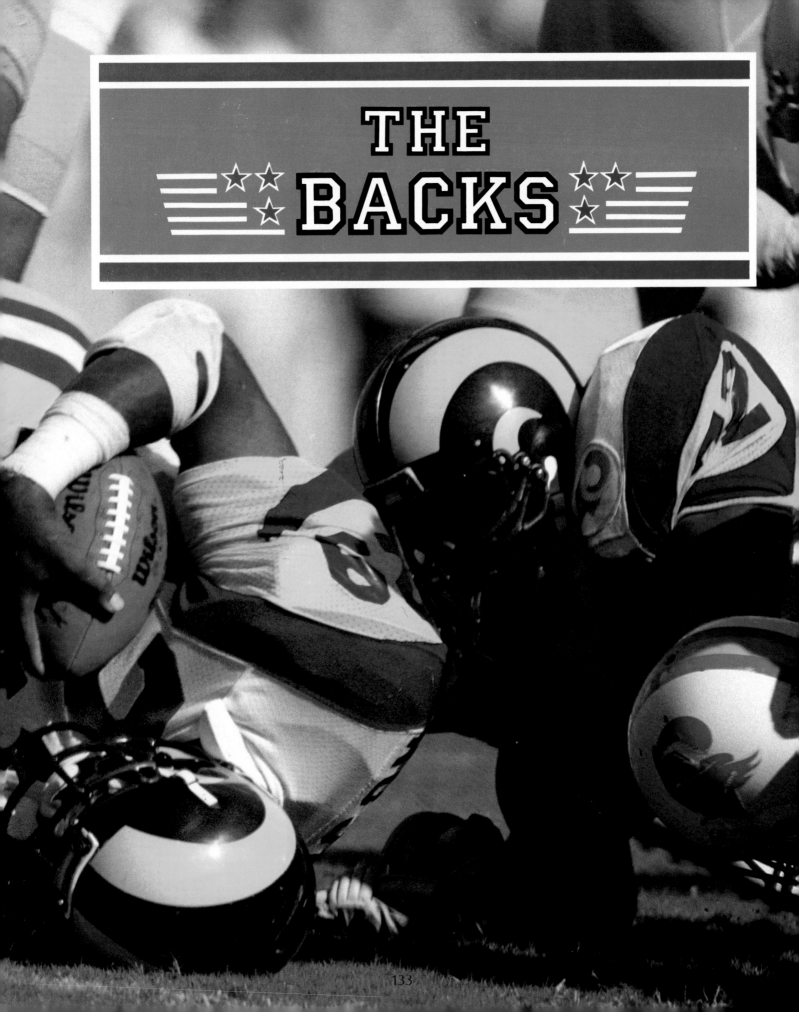

THE BACKS

Eric Dickerson

The scene was one right out of a Wild West shootout. Swaggering into town was Eric Dickerson, a Texas boy coming home as a star, glitzy credentials and all. Dickerson, in only his second season in the NFL, is on the verge of football history as he stalks O.J. Simpson's revered 2,003-yard season. Waiting in their own backyard is the Houston Oilers, a team of also-rans talking like stars. They were going to stop Dickerson they proclaimed. And stop him cold.

In the Houston papers the Oilers accused Dickerson of being an average Joe, just a role player lucky enough to be running behind the best offensive line in football.

"My friends back home called me and read what they were saying," recalls Dickerson about his record-breaking chase in 1984. "They said the line did most of the work and that I am just an average back.

"I wanted to prove them wrong. I was going to show them that not just one defensive back could bring me down."

Baiting Dickerson in the press was the first mistake the Oilers made. The second one was worse – baiting Dickerson while the game was in progress. That got Dickerson even angrier. Nostril-flaring angry. Bronco-busting angry. Record-breaking angry.

"I'm from the Houston area," Dickerson said. "When I was drafted, I said I didn't want to go to Houston. I didn't see that team going anywhere.

"A lot of them took that personally. They were out there today, talking at me, taking cheap shots. Really dirty things. On tackles, they'd twist my head, my knees, my ankles. I was getting ticked. I told them, 'It's gonna be rough on y'all today.'

"If I came up to a hole in the line, I was going to butt some heads. I was going to run some defensive backs over."

Like a good gunfighter, Dickerson was true to his word, making Houston eat the unkind words they spoke. Dickerson rushed for 215 yards that

Previous pages: Eric Dickerson is stopped by Tampa Bay's Ron Holmes. Dickerson (left and facing page) is the NFL's all-time single season rushing leader with 2,105 yards.

day, giving him 2,007 yards on the season, eclipsing O.J. Simpson's mark that experts felt would stand up like Joe DiMaggio's 56-game hitting streak. On the historic carry, number 27 on the day, Dickerson took a pitch and slashed off right tackle, breaking a couple of tackles before linebacker Gregg Bingham brought him down. It was a typical rush for Dickerson, making him the only other player besides Simpson to rush for 2,000 yards in a season.

Dickerson has developed into the star the Rams expected when they selected him with the number two pick in the 1983 draft. Dickerson, who teamed with New England's Craig James at Southern Methodist University in the Pony Express backfield, is a perfect combination of size, speed and strength. Not only could he run around tacklers, but as Houston found out, Dickerson could run through them.

That was established in his rookie campaign when Dickerson rushed for 1,808 yards, an unheard of figure for any runner, let alone a first-year player. Not only was his yardage an NFL rookie record, but so were his 18 touchdowns. He also led the NFL in carries with 390, showing his durability.

His first season was nothing compared to his second year, when Dickerson ripped through opposing defenses, averaging 5.6 yards per carry and 132 yards a game for 2,105 total yards.

"I can't define a weakness in Eric Dickerson," says former Eagles coach Dick Vermeil. "Although all great backs are multi-talented, most have one thing they do extremely well. But this guy can plow through a pile of bodies like (John) Riggins and then put on the moves like (Tony) Dorsett."

Coming into the 1985 campaign, Dickerson put the moves on the Rams, asking for a new, lucrative contract. The dispute raged for weeks with Dickerson holding out and missing training camp. Despite losing all that practice time, Dickerson finished '85 as the eighth leading

rusher in the league with 1,234 yards. Far below Dickerson's expectations, but outstanding for anyone else. Still, Dickerson is out to make 1986 his best season ever.

"People talk about the greatest runners," he said. "Some say Walter (Payton) is the best, some say O.J., some say me, some say Jim Brown. I just say I'm good."

The Houston Oilers will attest to that.

Marcus Allen

Ever since Marcus Allen entered the NFL as a first round draft pick of the Los Angeles Raiders in 1982, he's wanted to be a bigger part of the offense. Sure the Raiders have plenty of weapons, the long bomb or the sure over-the-middle pass to tight end Todd Christensen. But Marcus wanted to contribute more. Like the days at the University of Southern California where he won the Heisman Trophy and ran the ball 30 times a game.

But with the Raiders, Marcus had to adjust to being part of the offense, not the centerpiece. In his rookie season, the strike-shortened nine game year, Allen rushed for 697 yards on 160 carries, becoming the first rookie ever to lead the NFL in scoring with his 18 TDs. Still he averaged only 18 rushes per game. In 1983 and '84, Allen handled the ball about the same number of times with similar results, gaining 1,014 and 1,168 yards respectively. Still the former USC glamor boy wanted more.

"I still believe the more you get the ball, the better you get," Allen said. "I still feel that when you get into a groove, no matter who's up there (on the line), you can do something. You can create some yards. If you're not in the groove, it's kind of difficult."

"In the history of the Raiders, Marcus is the only halfback to gain 1,000 yards," says Allen's close friend O.J. Simpson. "It normally only happened at their fullback position because mostly all they do is drive block. They go for the big linemen to give them a good base for their pass blocking, but those huge guys work against you running the ball, especially for a halfback who's trying to get off-tackle or outside behind a pulling guard.

"A halfback would prefer to play for a team like the Rams or Dolphins, teams with excellent running schemes. The Raiders don't run traps well, nor are they the fastest offensive line in the league."

But with the Raiders in a semi-transition season and with starting quarterback Jim Plunkett out with an injury, Los Angeles succumbed to Allen's request last season with startling results.

Allen ran the ball 380 times in '85 tops in the American Football Conference, compared to his '84 total of 275 times. He responded with his greatest season, leading the NFL in rushing with 1,759 yards and scoring 11 touchdowns. He also hauled in 67 passes and, whenever teams played the Raiders, stopping Marcus Allen was the key to winning. With the Raiders 12-4 regular season record, not many teams found the key.

"He's a true halfback," says teammate Kenny King. "When I saw him play at USC, I thought, 'It's the offensive line.' But the first time I saw him run in camp, I knew it was Marcus Allen.

"He stops on a dime, takes off like a cat, spins. It looks like three or four yards, but he turns it into 16."

Never was that more evident in Allen's career than in the 1983 season, when he led the Raiders to a Super Bowl win over the Washington Redskins. Who can forget the greatest single play in Super Bowl history when Allen was trapped in the backfield, a certainty for a big yardage loss. Somehow Allen reversed his field, then ran 74 yards through the tough Redskins defense to record the longest rush from scrimmage in Super Bowl history. Of course he won the Super Bowl MVP trophy and his 191 yards are a Super Bowl record, but that one play highlighted the host of natural talents Marcus Allen possesses.

"When Marcus Allen graduated, he was the fifth-leading receiver in USC history," says John Robinson, former USC coach now head man with the Rams. "Obviously we used him a lot as a receiver. He's a great athlete."

"We felt he had the qualities we were looking for," says Raiders coach Tom Flores, who was instrumental in

The Jets' Freeman McNeil (above and facing page) is among the league's elite runners, although sometimes he doesn't get the credit. "He is the heart and soul of that offense," says Bob Griese. "You wonder why he's not always mentioned. Maybe he's just a blue-collar runner."

---

plucking Allen with the 10th pick in '82. "It makes him a pretty capable back when he can block, run and throw the option pass."

Now the Raiders have an option. With a healthy squad, they could return to the offensive scheme that was so successful before Allen, or they could keep Allen happy and give him the ball.

Either way, Marcus Allen proved his point to the Raiders and the rest of the league.

Freeman McNeil

Think of the best running backs in the NFL and the names Eric Dickerson, Walter Payton and Marcus Allen jump out at you. But if you think a little harder, there is one guy who is being left out. How about Freeman McNeil, the New York Jets outstanding running back who certainly belongs with the best the league has to offer.

"For people who really sit down and evaluate ballplayers and their importance, Freeman is recognized as a great one," says Hall-of-Fame defensive tackle Merlin Olsen. "Freeman's not a guy who blows his own horn. He also makes the difficult things look easy. That combination has denied him some of what he should have been accorded."

"If you've ever watched him, he is the heart and soul of that offense," says Bob Griese, former Miami quarterback, now a color commentator. "They throw to him and run with him. You wonder why he's not always mentioned. Maybe he's just a blue-collar runner."

There are several reasons why McNeil is often overlooked as one of the best in the business. The number one reason may be his running style. He's not a blur the way Eric Dickerson can be, leaving tacklers with incredible speed. He's not a power runner the way Walter Payton can be, punishing opponents with vicious stiff arms and head-butting collisions. In running styles, he's more like Marcus Allen. No blazing speed, no raw power to break tackles. McNeil can best be classified as a shifty runner, using a slashing style to leave tacklers grasping for something they can't find. He's like a magician. Now you have him, now you don't.

"One question everyone asked about his talent was whether he had enough speed," Olsen adds, "but it's not out-and-out pure speed that makes the difference. What he can do is go in five directions at the same time.

"He's a lot like Gale Sayers (Hall-of-Fame Bears running back). Gale would come right at you and if you didn't get both arms locked around him, he'd be gone."

"Freeman might not be a breakaway threat like some other guys, but he's got that slashing zig-zagging style," says Jets center Joe Fields. "Freeman won't break too many 80-yard runs, but he'll give you a lot of 25 and 30-yarders because of that slashing style."

And how. In 1985, McNeil led the Jets with 1,331 yards, good for second in the AFC and fifth best in the league. He did this despite rushing almost 100 less times than the NFL leader, Marcus Allen. Before he was injured in the eighth game, he topped the NFL rushers by a wide margin, averaging more than 118 yards per game. And since joining the Jets from UCLA as the third pick in the 1981 draft, McNeil has led the NFL in rushing (786 yards in the strike year), broken the Jets' records for yards in a season (last season) and been named to play in the Pro Bowl in three of the last four campaigns.

As an All-American at UCLA, McNeil broke the school record for most yards in a season (1,396) and in a career (3,195). Still, he doesn't get the respect others do. Perhaps it is the easy-going, low-key style the 27-year-old maintains.

"My talent is the total result of a team effort," he says. "It's not one man. I don't want to tell anybody how good I am. I thank God for my talent and that's what makes me humble. Some guys read about themselves so much to the point they don't think about the other 10 guys who are busting their butts. Everybody can do something better than I can."

Pittsburgh Steelers head coach Chuck Noll once said there are usually two types of runners; elusive runners and slashers. Freeman McNeil, he surmised, is an elusive slasher. McNeil seems to have a sixth sense, cutting at the precise time to avoid tacklers, making the best of even the slightest hole in the defense. He credits his success to preparation.

"I don't play the play, I play the game," he says. "That's the only way I can make things happen. When a block doesn't go a certain way, I know enough about the guy in front of me to make an adjustment. It becomes a reaction. I look for the open spot, and whatever I see I take.

"I want to be the best runner that my linemen ever blocked for. I'll be the last guy to come off the field. Walter Payton is one of the greatest examples, based on his mentality and his performances week-in and week-out. He's so consistent. He's setting a great example for the rest of us."

An example that Freeman McNeil is following perfectly.

Walter Payton

When O.J. Simpson set an all-time NFL record by rushing for 273 yards in a game, nobody thought it would ever be surpassed. The same things were said when Jim Brown finished his career in 1965 with 12,312 yards, the most in NFL history. Perhaps the same things will be said when Walter Payton retires, but for now, Payton is acknowledged as the greatest running back in NFL history. As Casey Stengel used to say, "You can look it up."

Entering his 12th season in the league, Payton has rushed for 14,860 yards. His 275 yards rushing the football against the Minnesota Vikings in 1977 is still a record. So is his 73 games with 100 yards rushing, his 3,371 attempts, his nine 1,000-yard rushing seasons and his most combined yards in a career. There are not many rushing records that Walter Payton doesn't own. But don't worry, he's still going strong at age 33.

He proved that last year when he led the Bears with 1,551 yards rushing to finish third in the NFL. He carried the ball over 300 times for the ninth time in his career. But perhaps the greatest accomplishment Payton has achieved is his durability. At a position with a life expectancy of three years, Payton has survived 11 seasons of constant contact, of butting heads with linebackers and taking on defensive backs instead of stepping out of bounds.

Walter Payton has missed just one game – as a rookie – out of 150 since he joined the Bears in 1975. He has started 143 straight games, a fantastic achievement if you're a punter, let alone someone who handles the ball 30 times a game. That record may be even more impressive than his gaudy rushing totals.

"It all starts with genetics," says Clyde Emrich, the Bears strength coach. "Any great athlete has to have the right body leverage for his sport. He has to have a better nervous system than most. And if his sport requires speed, strength and reaction time more than endurance, he has to have an abundance of fast-twitch cells in his muscles. He has to have excellent hand-eye coordination.

"When Walter went down the assembly line, everything was a chrome-plated part. It must have been like, 'Here comes Walter. Give me the top of the line.'"

If Payton hadn't decided to make it as a running back, he certainly could have starred as a quarterback or wide receiver. That's how much athletic ability the 5-10, 202-pound Payton has.

"He could play any position," says teammate Brian Baschnagel. "I think what amazes me most is, here's a running back who can throw the ball 100 yards. I think the most incredible

thing I've seen was the time he threw me a 50-yard touchdown pass. He was literally going down, and he not only had the strength to whip the ball that far sidearm, but also the presence of mind to realize he could do it."

"We get hundreds of calls from therapists, hypnotists, doctors," says Chicago trainer Fred Caito, "who want to cut him open and find out what's inside."

The Chicago management found out what's inside when they drafted Payton as the fourth pick in the 1974 draft. Although playing at little-known Jackson State, Payton made scouts drool despite finishing 12th in the Heisman Trophy voting behind Archie Griffin. They liked his speed, his strength and his attitude. As former Bears G.M. Jim Finks said at the draft, "We're not any cleverer than anybody else. A blind man could tell he was going to make it big."

And how. Payton started slowly in his rookie campaign, gaining only 679 yards on 196 carries. Omitting the strike-shortened 1982 season, it was the only year Payton did not gain 1,000 or more rushing.

"It would be so easy for someone with his ability to sit back and not work out much," Baschnagel says. "But he goes after every play as if it's the most important in his career."

"Walter still plays like he's trying to be the best tailback in the tenth grade," says Chicago defensive tackle Dan Hampton. "He still has the same enthusiasm."

That enthusiasm has remained intact because through all his accomplishments, with all his records and days of glory, the one thing Payton wanted more than any personal records was a championship. A Super Bowl ring. And, with the help of the Bears, he finally got it in 1985.

Now the all-time king of running backs is sitting on the throne, relaxed with the knowledge that he has accomplished his goal. And nobody deserves it more than Walter Payton.

Facing page: Walter Payton shows off the characteristic Payton stride (top) against the Patriots in the Super Bowl. One of the most durable backs ever, Payton has missed just one game out of 150 since he joined the Bears in 1973.

Tony Dorsett

You'd think after all these years, the defenses would be able to stop him. There's Tony Dorsett, 10 yards behind the line of scrimmage, hands on hips, looking as calm as if he were playing touch football in the park. Quarterback Danny White barks the signals and the ball is snapped. Dorsett, the Cowboys' all-time leading rusher, fakes left and veers right. White tosses the ball wide and Dorsett carefully tucks it away under his number 33 on his right hip.

His eyes are like a prison spotlight, scanning the field, searching for something that doesn't seem to be there. Dorsett's legs gracefully move him towards the line of scrimmage, blockers ahead of him trying to clear a path. A shoulder fake inside and the middle linebacker reacts, committing himself to the inside run. Dorsett heads for the hole on an apparent collision course with someone paid to knock off his head.

Just before impact, something happens. Actually, nothing happens. In a flash, Dorsett slithers outside, leaving the linebacker grabbing for something that's no longer there. In an instant, Dorsett is motoring up the sideline, juking and jitterbugging his way toward another 10-yard gain.

Such has been the outstanding career of Tony Dorsett, one of the few runners in NFL history to gain over 10,000 yards. Despite the big numbers, despite playing on America's Team and being on national television practically every week, Tony Dorsett is a poor man's Walter Payton.

Think of the great running backs of this era. Certainly there's Payton and Eric Dickerson and Earl Campbell. It's easy to forget Tony Dorsett. He never singlehandedly carried a team the way the others did. He also never had to, playing on a perennial winner in Dallas. But the statistics don't lie. Tony Dorsett will go down as one of the greatest running backs ever.

In his nine seasons in the NFL, Dorsett has gained over 1,000 yards each season except the strike-shortened 1982 campaign. He has been named to the Pro Bowl four times and each season Dorsett seems to become a bigger threat out of the backfield with his receiving ability. Still, recognition has not come easily for Dorsett. And it bothers him.

"I think I've accomplished a lot in my first nine years and have gradually moved up on the all-time rushing list, but I feel somewhat like Rodney Dangerfield. I don't get the kind of respect that I merit. When it's all over and done, I'll be sitting up there pretty high on the all-time list. But what are people going to think of my accomplishments? I don't know.

"I haven't seen a back yet that I didn't feel I could be as productive as. In Chicago, they run all the time and they've got those big hogs (linemen) up there. Walter (Payton) can pick his hole and run. Same thing out in L.A. with Eric (Dickerson). Those guys are exceptional athletes, but you can see what they are working with. You put a guy like Charles White, who was just about out of football last year, behind that L.A. line and you see what happens. I feel I can do just as good or better than anybody else if I was working under the same conditions."

The conditions Dorsett works

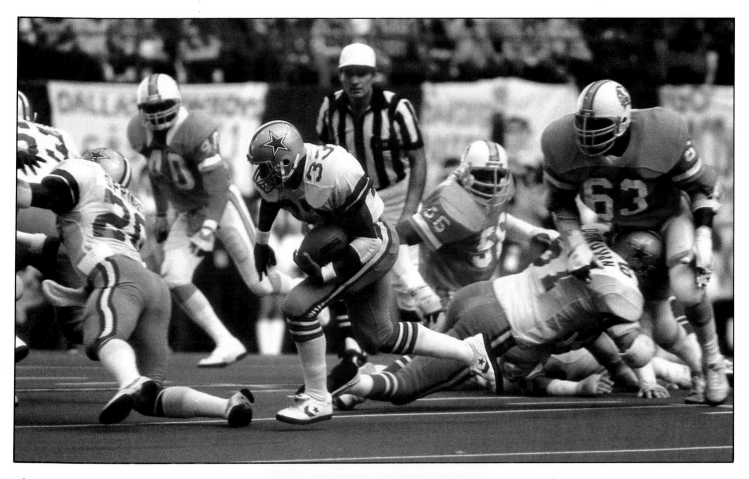

Like Freeman McNeil, sometimes Tony Dorsett doesn't get the recognition he deserves. For years he has haunted the Washington Redskins (right and facing page) in the clashes between the two teams. Dorsett's slashing style (above) has produced 1,000-yard seasons eight times in his career, including four years when he has been named to the Pro Bowl. And, at age 32, Dorsett seems to be getting better. In 1985 he rushed for 1,307 yards, placing him sixth in the league. "His greatest asset is his quickness and speed," says former Cowboy coach Dan Reeves.

under are the constraints put on him by coach Tom Landry. The Cowboys run a diversified offense, mixing passing and running, limiting the number of carries for Dorsett. In fact in his nine seasons in the league, Dorsett has averaged only 18 carries per game, well below the average for Dickerson or Payton.

The limited workload has also produced a positive effect, something Landry had in mind when the Cowboys selected the former Heisman Trophy winner with the second pick in the 1976 draft. Dorsett, now the oldest running back in the

league at age 32, has stayed away from serious injuries, such as the one that prematurely ended Billy Sims' career last season.

"It seems everybody does have injuries," Dorsett says, referring to the injuries to Sims, Seattle's Curt Warner and Atlanta's William Andrews. "I have been lucky and I don't like to think about something negative like that happening to me. But I'm also realistic. It is the nature of the business and you can be wiped out on a given play at any given time."

Luckily for the Cowboys that hasn't happened, allowing Dorsett to continue using his greatest asset, his speed and quickness, throughout his career. In fact, Dorsett doesn't seem to be slowing down. In 1985, the Rochester, Pennsylvania native rushed for 1,307 yards to finish sixth in the NFL.

"His greatest asset is his quickness and speed," says former Dallas assistant coach Dan Reeves, now the head man in Denver. "Like Walter Payton, he has so much talent."

Now if only his recognition matched his talent.